A WAR JOURNAL OF

THE FIFTH (KENYA) BATTALION

THE KING'S AFRICAN RIFLES

The Naval & Military Press Ltd

Reproduced by kind permission of the Central Library,
Royal Military Academy, Sandhurst

Published by
The Naval & Military Press Ltd
Unit 10, Ridgewood Industrial Park,
Uckfield, East Sussex,
TN22 5QE England
Tel: +44 (0) 1825 749494
Fax: +44 (0) 1825 765701
www.naval-military-press.com
www.military-genealogy.com

© The Naval & Military Press Ltd 2007

The Naval & Military Press ...

...offer specialist books for the serious student of conflict. The range of titles stocked covers the whole spectrum of military history with titles on uniforms, battles, official histories, specialist works containing Medal Rolls and Casualties Lists, and numismatic titles for medal collectors and researchers.

The innovative approach they have to military bookselling and their commitment to publishing have made them Britain's leading independent military bookseller.

In reprinting in facsimile from the original, any imperfections are inevitably reproduced and the quality may fall short of modern type and cartographic standards.

FOREWORD

By

Major-General C. C. Fowkes, C.B.E., D.S.O., M.C.

I esteem it a great honour to be asked to write a Foreword for this War Journal of the 5th (K) Battalion The Kings African Rifles.

I brought up two battalions of the old Southern Brigade from Tanganyika in October 1939, and the Fifth then in Nanyuki joined us to form the 2nd, later the 22nd E. A. Brigade. I suspected that this new association was not altogether to their liking but it was an association in which we marched together from N.F.D. to the "Chindwin".

Both the authors of this Journal took a leading part in the deeds they describe and have shown a becoming modesty in retailing them, but from the early anxious days at "Moyale" through the campaign in Italian Somaliland and Abyssinia until they finally came to rest at "Gimma" the Fifth progressively showed themselves the loyal, tough, hard fighting Battalion on which a Commander is only too glad to depend.

After these years of fighting in Africa, it was only natural that when told by 14th Army to provide myself with a Reconnaissance Battalion I should bethink myself of my old comrades in the Fifth. I seem to remember that my first requests for their services met with considerable resistance, but my pleadings at length prevailed and they joined us in the "Kabaw Valley".

There was to be very little "reconnaissance" in the role they were called upon to play. The strong Japanese posts at "Letsegan" flanking as it did our main line of advance was a constant threat to our communication. The country was really terrible but I felt that if anyone could destroy this mountain fortress it was the Fifth. So off they went and did the job, and well I remember the sigh of relief in our Divisional Headquarters, both for their sakes and our own when we heard the tidings of their gallant achievements.

The War Story of the Fifth is a splendid example of what can be achieved by a well lead, well trained K. A. R. Battalion with a generous leavening of that fine product of East Africa, the disciplined long service Askari.

The Fifth much I am sure to their disappointment have not been selected for service in Malaya, but their turn may come and we may rest assured that they will gallantly maintain the tradition of those whose deeds are described in this Journal.

AUTHOR'S PREFACE.

This Journal, a record of the Battalion during the War of 1939 — 1945 compiled from official documents or notes made at the time, is intended primarily to be of interest to those who served with the Battalion during that period.

It contains light hearted passages, comments, and criticisms, out of place in a more serious work, which it is hoped will help to recall to readers the days they spent in service with the Battalion.

The Authors hope that this record may also be of interest to those who now serve or will hereafter serve with the Battalion and an endeavour has been made to present a faithful picture of the difficulties with which the Battalion had to contend.

They wish to express their thanks to Mr. J.W. Howard for the loan of his manuscript dealing with the campaign in Abyssinia from which much has been extracted verbatim; to Major D. Dewar of the Military Records Office, Nairobi, for valuable assistance in the preparation of the Appendices and other material, and to Lt. Col. H. Moyse-Bartlett for information on the early history of the Battalion.

W. D. Draffan.
T. C. C. Lewin.

CONTENTS

CHAPTER 1.	Introduction, 1899 — 1939.
CHAPTER 2.	Mobilisation and Training.
CHAPTER 3.	Operations in Kenya.
CHAPTER 4.	Conquest of Italian Somaliland.
CHAPTER 5.	The advance to Addis Ababa.
CHAPTER 6.	The battle of the lakes.
CHAPTER 7.	The campaign in Madagascar.
CHAPTER 8.	Interlude.
CHAPTER 9.	Burma — west of the Chindwin.
	Part 1. The Approach March.
	Part 2. The action at Letsegan.
	Part 3. Nyaungbin to the Chindwin.
	Part 4. Operations of Drafforce.
	Part 5. Operations of "C" Company.
CHAPTER 10.	Burma — East of the Chindwin.
CHAPTER 11.	Assam and Bengal.

APPENDICES.
1. Adjutant's Battle Log. (Letsegan).
2. Extracts from Army Commander's Address.
3. Divisional Commander's Farewell Letter.
4. Officer Commanding.

MAPS.
1. East Africa.
2. Madagascar.
3. Burma — Kabaw Valley.

CHAPTER I.

INTRODUCTION. 1899 — 1939.

Curiously enough the 5th K.A.R. was originally an Indian Unit, which was sent from India to help quell the mutiny of Sudanese troops which broke out in Uganda in September 1897.

Two drafts of two hundred men each were sent from India to serve a tour in Uganda and were known as the "Uganda Indian Contingent". Fear of another uprising led to the continuation of this policy and as the drafts became time expired other drafts of equal strength were sent from India to Uganda to replace them.

When all troops in East and Central Africa were re-organised into the Kings African Rifles on 1st January 1902 this Uganda Indian Contingent was re-named the 5th (Uganda) Bn. K.A.R. In all there were six battalions but because the 5th were Indian they took precedence. The battalion consisted of four companies of one hundred men each with seven officers. The Commanding Officer was Major M. L. Hornby D.S.O. (Indian Staff Corps).

In 1904, the former Eastern Province of Uganda was transferred to British East Africa (as Kenya Colony was then known) and it was decided to halve the strength of the Indian Battalion. The 5th K.A.R. was accordingly disbanded and the 4th K.A.R. instead of being purely African became seven African and two Indian Companies. This original 5th K.A.R. never served outside Uganda.

The Battalion was raised again in 1916 during the expansion of the K.A.R. It was the only Battalion to remain a single battalion as it was intended for duty in Jubaland and the Northern Frontier District where it fought a tedious campaign against one Abduraman Marsaal who had raised his standard in revolt. The battalion was made up from the former Camel Company of the 3rd K.A.R. then in Jubaland, one and a half companies of the 3rd K.A.R. in the Northern Frontier District, men from the Police Service Battalion, then being disbanded, Somali and other recruits from irregular forces. The Commanding Officer was Lt. Col. W. E. H. Barrett (Reserve of Officers) whose appointment dated from 1st June 1916. Thus the Battalion never fought against the Germans in the 1914-1918 War.

After the War the 5th K. A. R., alternating with the 3rd K.A.R., were stationed at Meru and resposible for the peace and security of both The Northern Frontier District and Jubaland combining the duties of soldiers, policeman and administrators. On the 26th January 1924 the two Battalions (the 3rd and the 5th) were presented with their colours by His Excellency Sir Robert Coryndon, Governor and Commander in Chief Kenya.

In February 1925 the Battalion carried out a punitive expedition against the Mohamed Zubir section of the Somalis who had mustered about 5,000 men in revolt. After inflicting some fifty casualties and capturing about 20,000 head of stock the revolt was squashed.

By now the arrangements for the hand over to Italy of Jubaland were complete and on June 29th 1925 Italy took formal possession thus relieving the K.A.R., of this commitment. As a direct result, on the grounds of economy, the Battalion was disbanded in June of the following year, and handed their Colours to their sister Battalion the 3rd for safe custody. Four years later the Battalion was again reformed, this time to be brigaded with the 3rd and 4th (Uganda) to form the Northern Brigade and on 1st March 1930 their old Colours were re-presented by his Excellency Sir Edward Grigg, Governor and Commander in Chief.

It was now that the Regimental March (recently jettisoned for the popular marching song "Tufunge Safari") was composed by Bandmaster Bowler and the African Band-Sergeant from an old native melody which accounted for its distinctive character.

From its re-embodiment in 1930 to 1936 the Battalion was stationed at Nairobi for garrison duties, which appear to have included operations against the locust invasion, but on two occasions detachments were sent to the Northern Frontier, one to Meru and the other to Lokitaung, to assist in operations. The detachment sent to Lokitaung took part in what was at the time considered a large scale operation in the almost un-administered south east corner of the Sudan. The operations are of interest as they were the first to be mechanised. Prior to this troops had operated in the desert areas with pack camels or ox wagons. The detachment travelled from Nairobi by lorry, joined the Lokitaung garrison of the 4th K.A.R., and moved north to Lokitoi. The force of two companies with Vickers M.M.Gs. lashed to the lorries and escorted by several hundred Turkhana tribesmen, descended to the plains north of Lorienatom where an engagement was fought against the Merille. Heavy casualties were inflicted and many cattle recovered at Lomwanagippi. The detachment remained in the Kaithrin Lorienatom hills for six months before moving to Todenyang on Lake Rudolph and thence back to Nairobi to rejoin the Battalion.

CHAPTER 2.

MOBILISATION AND TRAINING.

In 1931 the old light blue flash was discarded in favour of the present dark blue flash and in the same year it was decided to cease recruitment of Somali. Recruitment into the Battalion was then chiefly from Nandi, Kipsigis and Kamba but in 1936 recruitment of Somali again started.

In 1936 the Battalion relieved the 3rd K.A.R. at Meru but were not destined to remain there for long, for on the construction of the new barracks at rail-head at Nanyuki the Battalion moved thence early in 1939.

Thus it was at Nanyuki on the 26th August 1939 that the Battalion received orders to mobilise for the Second World War.

Mobilisation procceded smoothly, the Colours and Officers Mess Silver being despatched to a Nairobi Bank for safe custody. Re-enforcements of Officers and N. C. O's., drawn for the most part from the Kenya Regiment, though a few officers were posted from the K. A. R. Reserve of Officers, arrived by the end of the month.

The mobilisation plan, in the event of hostilities with Italy, visualised the Battalion moving to a battle station in the Isiola area and accordingly on the 2nd September the Battalion left Nanyuki by motor transport for Isiola.

This transport was almost entirely commandeered African and Indian buses and lorries, most in a dubious state of repair. These vehicles came straight off the roads were given a quick inspection by a much over-worked M.T. staff and if they looked capable of getting as far as Isiola they were impressed. In the event very few failed to make the trip and quite a number remained with the Battalion for a long time.

At the time of mobilisation "D" Coy, Captain J.A.H. Powell, was stationed at Wajir with one platoon at Moyale and another at Mandera. The Administration decided to evacute these two out-posts and the platoons were withdrawn back to Wajir; meanwhile Lieut. Trent with a platoon from "C" coy was sent off to Garissa to guard the aerodrome and a small detachment sent to Merti to give early warning of an enemy advance. This out-post not being aware of the withdrawal of the Administration from Moyale and having been warned that any vehicles approaching from the North were likely to be enemy mistook the D. C.'s safari, approaching in the dusk with their lights on for the Italians, and withdrew to another position to await the dawn and the enemy. This was an unhappy incident with which to start a war but perhaps the District Commissioner has reason to be glad of the inexperience which lead to this unwarranted withdrawal. A more resolute commander would no doubt have fired first and asked afterwards.

As is now known the Italians did not enter the war for another nine months and so on 12th August "C" Coy (Capt. Kemble) were ordered to re-occupy Moyale, which in the meantime had been thoroughly looted of any material left behind by the Administration.

The position now was Battalion Headquarters and Two Companies at Isiola, with one company forward at Wajir and another at Moyale and thus they awaited the onslaught of the Italians who were known to have something approaching fifty brigades in East Africa. As the Battalion were at the time the only troops in the whole of the Northern Frontier, and were armed with nothing more lethal than four Vickers Machine Guns, one Bren gun late of the Abyssinian Army and still bearing the insignia of the Lion of Judah, with a majority of its Lewis Guns clearly marked "Drill Purposes", it was as well that the onslaught never materialised.

While at Isiola Lt. Col. Barkas, Capt. R.A.F. Hurt and Capt. Tweedie all returned from leave, the Colonel taking over command from Major J.S. Hewick who reverted to Second in Command, Capt. Tweedie taking over Adjutant from Lt. D. M. Geddes, and Capt. Hurt taking over his old "A" Coy.

In the middle of August the Battalion less the two forward Companies and the one Platoon at Isiola, returned to Nanyuki for training. Later the forward Companies were relieved by other troops and the Battalion was again complete.

As was mentioned earlier in this Chapter the Battalion British personnel had been brought up to War Establishment by re-inforcements from the Reserve of Officers and from the Kenya Regiment. These Officers and N. C. O's though filled with enthusiasm had as yet little training and a special cadre under the direction of Major J. S. Hewick was started. A few precious Bren Guns arrived and the Machine Gun Platoon, which had been sent under Lt. E. de Las Casas to join a Machine Gun Battalion formed round the 3rd K.A.R. in Nairobi, was replaced by a 3" Mortar Platoon. This Platoon was formed mainly from elements of the old Machine Gun Platoon which had not gone with the rest to Nairobi, supported by the best riflemen in the Battalion. Training of the Platoon proceeded smoothly until aiming instruction was reached when it was found that not a man in the Platoon could read the dial sight. On investigation it was found they could not read the slide of the backright on their Lee Enfields rifles either and adjusted their sights by counting the lines. So all had to go to School. Came the great day when they were judged fit to fire a practice bomb and the whole Battalion turned out to witness this historic event—the first Mortar to be fired in East Africa. Away went the first bomb to land reasonably close to the target, adjustments were ordered and away went the second to land within fifty yards of a well known resident's house. At this juncture the C.O. was heard to murmur he "hoped there was not going to be an incident". The third and last bomb did land where it was intended.

Respirator, Capes anti-gas and similar novelties were issued at this time and did not prove popular as it became the habit to march the last four miles uphill into the barracks wearing the respirator. At the end of twelve to fifteen miles in the African sun this was not pleasant.

Down on the plains below Nanyuki the M.T. Staff were busy training drivers in Convoy Drill and gradually the chaos which attended the Battalion's first move by Motor Transport began to give way to the disciplined movements which were later to become such a feature of the advance into Abyssinia.

Meanwhile the Southern Brigade of the K.A.R. (The 1st, 2nd and 6th Battalions) had moved up to Kenya and the 5th K.A.R. doubled up in its quarters at Nanyuki to house the 6th which arrived at the end of the year, the 1st K.A.R. taking over garrison duties in the Northern Frontier. The 1st, 5th and 6th Battalions were then Brigaded together under Brigadier C.C. Fowkes who established his Headquarters at the Nanyuki Sports Club just below the cantoonment area.

In January 1940 Brigade training started in the Isiola area, under the direction of the Brigadier who spared us nothing. This training was all by "march route" and day after day in the blazing sun the Battalions marched across the abombinable lava strewn terrain that exists in that area. None who took part in those exercises will lightly forget "Lava ridge" the scene of many bloodless battles or Shaffa Dinka of evil memory. But if the training was severe it was good and at its end all ranks were physically fit — apart perhaps from a few blisters — and full of confidence.

It is perhaps worth nothing that during these exercises the Askari of the King's African Rifles were put into boots for the first time in their history. It was generally held this was a mistake, that it would "slow them up", that they would get soft feet and so on. In fact it was a very wise order, and although at first there were a number of blistered feet it very soon turned out that foot casualties from thorns and stones were completely eliminated and there was no apparent loss of speed across country.

The early onset of the rains brought the exercises to an abrupt stop, much to the relief of the rank and file, and

for a short time there was risk of a serious food shortage owing to the supply route back to rail head being cut by the rains. The rains did, in fact, cause two casualties in the 4th Battalion K.A.R. who were camped on the Isiola River Heavy rains up in the hills brought the river down in spate during the night washing away an occupied tent and drowning two of the inmates.

Directly after the exercise the Battalion was stationed once again at Isiola, which indeed saved it a fifty mile march back to Nanyuki. From there all non-regular officers were posted to the second course at the recently established "School of Instruction" Nakuru for further general training.

While at Isiola the Battalion had its first War-time experience of a full scale Brigade Commander's inspection from which it emerged shaken but complete.

The Army in East Africa was beginning to take shape, the 22nd Mountain Battery from India had arrived and troops from the Gold Coast and from South Africa were preparing to sail. The K.A.R. itself was expanding fast, and ancillary Units such as the E.A. Reconnaissance Squadron, the East African Light Battery, Medical and Transport Units had been formed. From Rhodesia came an Armoured Car Unit. Stores and equipment of all kinds were arriving from the United Kingdom and from South Africa. No longer was one ill equipped battalion required to hold the Highland Fort. As the rains abated and the roads to the North dried out the Battalion with the bulk of the Brigade moved North and occupied the wells at Arbo just South of Wajir. There it remained practising "bush warfare" until the Italians declared War in June 1940.

CHAPTER 3

OPERATIONS IN KENYA

First blood went to the Italians. A working party from "A" Coy were on the landing ground near the Fort at Wajir when one of the Hawker Harts from the South African Air Force landed from a routine reconnaissance flight. Behind this rather old fashioned machine came three more aircraft which the troops took to be friendly but were in fact Italian Caproni Bombers almost as ancient as the Hart.

Caught in the open by this unexpected attack five were killed and fourteen wounded, while the R.A.F. petrol dump of 6,000 gallons was blown up. This incident had a telling effect on African morale and for sometime after they were nervous of any aircraft.

But if the Italians took the initiative in the air the Battalion took it on the ground and within a few days of Italy's entry into the war a Patrol from "A" Coy (Capt R. A. F. Hurt) contacted the enemy at Dif, a border post, and after a short skirmish drove out the enemy and returned with prisoners and information.

The next operation was against the enemy held border post of El Wak which was known to be one of their major positions along the Kenya—Italian Somaliland frontier but the actual strength was unknown. This operation was carried out by a composite force from both the 1st and 5th K.A.R. under the command of Capt. J. MacNab of the First. The main bulk of the force of two companies moved by a night compass march to the frontier, which is marked by a wide trace cut in the bush by the boundary commission, while a small supporting force of infantry and mortars moved by road in motor transport to an agreed Rendezvous on the left blank. At first light the two forces closed in on their objectives while a Reconnaissance Aircraft of the South African Air Force flew a sortie over the enemy position.

After opening fire on the aircraft, which received a bullet through its radiator and had eventually to land and be destroyed, the enemy totally unaware of the approach of ground forces, carried out their Air Raid Precautions Scheme by evacuating their camp for the Bush. Thus on the arrival of our troops they found the camp empty, to which, having salved documents and papers from the office and the wines from the mess, they set fire. The force then withdrew to the R.V. to await the transport. At this point the Italians returned and finding their camp on fire attacked the force with considerable vigour, and, having achieved surprise, effectively. After the first initial shock of this surprise attack our troops rallied and made a fighting withdrawal but had unfortunately to abandon the captured mess wines. This withdrawal was very gallantly supported by the unarmoured vehicles of the E.A. Reconnaissance Squadron.

The Battalion casualties were one one African killed and three wounded. Italian casualties were unknown. Shortly after this operation Lt. Col. Barkas had to relinquish command of the Battalion on medical grounds, Major J. D. de la M. Herapath assuming command.

The Italians were now showing fight and pressing the Moyale garrison hard, and on relief at Wajir by the 1st Gold Coast Battalion, the 5th K.A.R. moved north to try and relieve the pressure, establishing their Headquarters at Fanyanvatta about seven miles South of Moyale. After reconnaissance and a general survey of the situation the Brigade Commander decided that the enemy was in too great strength to hope for any chance of a permanent success and the decision to evacuate Moyale for the second time was made. Capt. Hurt ("A" Coy) and Capt Stopford ("D" Coy) who both knew Moyale well took their Companies close up to the defences but owing to poor communications the besieged force never received the evacuation order and the Companies had to withdraw under fire from both sides. The next day the message did get through and during the night a successful evacuation was made, the troops, carrying their arms and equipment, walking barefoot down the fixed lines of their own fire plan. In order to avoid giving away their intention to withdraw, no fires had been made but as much equipment and foodstuffs as possible had been destroyed by other means, however, to complete the destruction a Junkers Bomber of the South African Air Force flew over and bombed the fort. On its return the aircraft flew low over the Battalion at perhaps 100 feet. This proved too much for the nerves of a private in the Reconnaissance Squadron who opened up with his rifle. This action incited the nearby askari who also fired and despite the efforts of the officers to stop it a considerable volume of small arms fire was directed at the aircraft. The aircraft did not appreciate this attention and circling the camp area opened with its machine guns. In fact no casualties were caused on either side, except for a few holes in the aircraft.

From Fanyanyatta the Battalion withdrew to the Wells at Dobel, en route for Buna. During the march it was harassed by a ground straffing Savoia of the Italian Regia

Aeronautica. Coming up from behind it took the battalion by surprise and was gone before any effective fire could be opened. It was foolish enough to attempt the same manoeuvre on its return trip but by now the Battalion was ready and waiting. Flying so low that the faces of the pilot and gunners were clearly visible it swept down the road to be met by the concentrated fire of all automatics that could be brought to bear. Its wreckage was found later by a patrol some miles from the place of the incident.

The following day the withdrawal to Buna continued where the Battalion settled down in a Brigade Perimeter Camp. After some little time in this camp, which was sniped every now and then by the enemy's light forces and bombed by the Regia Aeronautica, a fighting patrol from the Nigerian Regt. attacked the enemy who had by now occupied Dobel. This attack was carried out with great gallantry by the Nigerians but was repulsed with heavy losses. As a result patrols from "A" Coy (Capt. Duirs) and later "C" Coy (Capt. Kemble) were sent forward to establish the enemy strength and dispositions at Dobel and Korondil. Although there were signs of recent enemy occupation at Korondil no enemy was found except a stray patrol of Banda which was attacked and driven off, but Dobel was found to be heavily defended by what appeared to be a battalion. Considerable credit is due to the Dobel patrol which lay up close to the enemy position throughout the whole day keeping it under close observation. It brought back also the identity discs of several Nigerian Askari which were lying unburied in the bush.

By now the Battalion had been in the bush for the best part of a year, living hard and without cover except the meagre shade of a thorn tree, or a ground sheet. Their resistance to disease began to fail. In the comparatively close confines of the perimeter camp dysentry began to appear and soon was rampant throughout the Battalion. The Battalion was therefore evacuated to fresh ground a few miles south of Buna in an effort to stem the disease. Although this action was effective it was decided to pull the Battalion out of the line for a rest and in September they moved back to Nanyuki via Arbajahan and Habbaswein. Six weeks rest at Nanyuki put the Battalion on its feet again and at the end of October they left for Marsabit. "C" Coy being stationed at North Horr and "D" Coy at Kalacha.

The task of the Battalion was now to prevent any enemy advance or infiltration through the Western edge of the

Northern Frontier Province and so to Archer's Post in rear of the troops in the Wajir area. Thus the operations were confined to frequent patrols to keep touch and gain information of the enemy and his intentions. The Battalion remained at Marsabit carrying out these wearisome but important duties until ordered to Garissa early in December.

It is now opportune to give a brief summary of the war situation in East Africa so that the future operations of the Battalion may be seen against the general pattern of events.

Moyale had fallen to the Italians in July and in August they had attacked and captured, with it must be admitted considerable skill and elan, British Somaliland. In September they occupied Buna which our forces had evacuated with the approach of the short rains. To the East the enemy made no advance and remained static, except for a little patrol activity, poised along the Kenya—Italian Somaliland Border with their main bases on the line of the Juba River, the fort of Afmadu covering the approaches to Kismayu, being a prominent exception. At the end of September 1940 therefore the intiative still rested with the enemy and why they never attempted an invasion of Kenya has not been satisfactorily explained. It is customary to explain this away as mere lack of enterprise and martial ardour but it is for far more probable that, being short of transport and fuel, and, so long as the Allied Forces retained command of the sea, little likelihood of replenishment, the wastes of the Northern Frontier provided too formidable an administrative barrier. It may be that they also appreciated that even if they succeeded in occupying Kenya the battle would continue in the south against ever increasing forces. In Europe the War had gone well for the Axis and no doubt they felt that victory there was assured and in due course they would receive a share of East Africa as part of the spoils of war, without the unpleasant necessity of fighting for it. But it has been suggested that "faint heart" may be the answer. Be that as it may they made no serious attempt at invasion.

In Kenya the armed forces had been building up rapidly. A Nigerian and a Gold Coast Brigade had arrived from the West Coast, while from the South had come the 1st Battalion The Northern Rhodesia Regt. and three Brigades of South Africans. From the South too had come Field Artillery, Light Tanks and Armoured Cars to re-inforce the units raised locally. These forces had been grouped into three Divisions, the 1st South African Division under Major-

General Brink (2nd S.A. Bn·, 5th S.A. Bde, 25th E.A. Bde) were holding the North West flank of the front, The 12th East African Division under Major-General Godwin-Austin (1st S.A. Bde, 22 E.A. Bde of which the 5th formed part, and the 24th Gold Coast Bde) held the centre, while the 11th East African Division, Major General Wetherall (23rd Nigerian Bde and 1st Northern Rhodesian Regiment) held the South-East. In all 22 Battalions of infantry with supporting arms. Between the two opposing forces lay a no-man's land of desert some eighty to one hundred miles in width.

In North Africa General Wavell was about to launch his campaign against the Italians on the Egyptian border and he directed that in Kenya, the East African Forces should close the gap between them and the enemy and regain the initiative prior to a general advance. Now followed a dramatic event which was to have an immense effect on the whole conduct of the Abyssinian Campaign. Major-General Godwin-Austin commanding the 12th E.A. Division and fresh from the evacuation of British Somaliland sensing that his troops had been on the defensive for too long decided that as a preliminary he must stage a decisive victory to restore the offensive spirit. He proposed therefore to launch the best part of his command against Buna (5th K.A.R. being at that time at Marsabit were not available) and detailed plans including air reconnaissance and special maps were prepared· Little more than a fortnight before the date of the proposed operation the Italians evacuated the objective. The plan was immediatly switched to an attack on El Wak, previously attacked by the 5th and 1st K.A.R., and an officer from the Fifth serving temporarily of the Divisional Staff was detailed to cut out of the bush between Wajir and Habbaswein a replica of the roads and tracks leading to the El Wak position. On this "practice course" as many of the troops as possible were exercised and on the 16th December the attack was launched. The enemy, believing that nothing more than a Battalion could possibly reach them, were taken completely by surprise and totally overwhelmed by the attack of the two brigades, supported by Aircraft, Artillery, Tanks and Armoured Cars. It really was a little hard on them· Fifteen guns, some hundred or so prisoners and above all secret document including the cypher books and general defense plan for Italian Somaliland were captured.

This swift and sudden disaster to the enemy forces appeared to destroy their morale, particularly as the Battalion stationed at El Wak was one of many similar Colonial

Infantry Battalions on which they were relying for the defence of Italian Somaliland. As a result the enemy withdrew all their forces, except the Afmadu garrison behind the line of the Juba River, and in the end made little or no attempt to stem the advance of the East African Forces. On the side of the East African forces the plan to close the gap gave way to that of a more immediate general advance.

CHAPTER 4.

CONQUEST OF ITALIAN SOMALILAND.

The Battalion arrived at Garissa early in December 1940 and all that month and most of January 1941 were waiting, first under 11 (EA) Div and later under 12 (EA) Div for the advance to begin.

Battalion Headquarters were West of the Tana River but the companies were much dispersed. "A" Coy formed the bridgehead over the Tana at Garissa. Here there was an intricate wiring and minefield system which did considerable damage to local camels and elephants. The civil Police Officer's house could only be approached by a narrow lane through the mine fields providing something of a hazard by night. "B" Coy were forward at Hagadera giving protection to a South African Road Construction Company. "C" Coy, when they arrived from Kalacha on 12th December, strengthened the Garissa bridgehead, and "D" Coy arriving on the 14th took over the Accra Bridgehead about a mile upstream from Garissa. In addition an outpost was stationed at Lamancha Sheik Hassan 25 miles South East. A notable mechanised patrol under Capt. Hughes-Young was sent to Jara Jila via the little known water pan of El Ein, to ascertain if this was a practicable route to the border and to report on water facilities. Arrived at El Ein to find the pan absolutely dry, the armoured cars with a somali guide tried to push on through dense bush — known as the El Ein thicket. After some hours with the armoured cars using a gallon of water a mile the point of no return was reached. The somali guide insisted there was ample water at Jara Jila — he had said the same of El Ein — but could give no indication of the distance. The patrol deciding that the route certainly was not practicable for formed bodies of troops returned without reaching their objective.

The plans for the advance were well kept and the Battalion believed that due to water shortage a limited advance only could be made until the rains had come again, and refilled the water pans, which were now rapidly drying out. As we have seen this indeed was the original intention until the sack of El Wak on the 16th altered the picture. The road makers had been busy preparing a magnificent road from Garissa to Haga Dera but no further; This too deceived the Battalion as well as the enemy into believing that no general advance would take place until the roads had been made ready, plainly a big job and an advance to Liboi on the frontier would be a preliminary for this task. In the event the bull-dozers followed close behind the leading troops and well in advance of the main body.

On January 12th "B" Coy was withdrawn from Haga Dera and rejoined the Battalion then at Mile 8 on the Garissa—Liboi road. It was evident that an advance was imminent. At 06.30 Hrs. on 23rd of January 1941 the advance, which was to continue practically without check to Addis Ababa 650 air miles to the North but double that distance by road, commenced. That night the 22nd E.A. Bde was concentrated in the Wardeglo area, 30 miles North East of Haga Dera, with "C" Coy and the Armoured Cars in the lead. Large numbers of Somali and their stock were found in the area but after a few choice words from the Brigadier they dispersed. That night intelligence reported a post of about 50 Banda at Liboi and a considerable force at Hawina some 30 miles further on.

Early next morning the Battalion in the same order continued the advance. The road runs through thick bush sandy underfoot, passing about half way to Liboi, an open patch made some time before to rescue an aircraft of the South African Air force which had force landed. At Liboi there were two main water pans, but neither of them held as much as the Wardeglo pan.

The first opposition was encountered between the two pans. A few hand grenades were thrown at the leading armoured cars but when the troops debussed the enemy soon cleared off and the main Liboi water hole was occupied by 09.45 Hrs.

Armoured Car Patrols were pushed forward and the remainder of the Battalion came up to Liboi. Half way between Liboi and the border cut the Armoured Cars ran into courageous resistance from the Banda, the leading car falling into a tank trap constructed by Lieut di Boli, commander of the Banda Sotto Gruppo. This was soon hauled out and the advance guard proceeded to the boundary cut where they consolidated. Later in the day the Armoured Cars went on down the camel track in thick bush to Dobli but no further opposition was encountered. That night the whole Battalion, with Brigade Headquarters and attached troops bivouaced on the boundary cut.

The resistance during the day had been slight but nevertheless some of the most courageous encountered at any time during the advance. About 50 Bande, mostly of the Mohamed Zubir Section of Somalis, an ancient enemy of the 5th K.A.R., armed with Breda Hand Grenades and rifles against a Brigade with strong supporting arms and proceeded by Armoured Cars. The latter were undoubtedly the weapon most feared by the enemy, and all prisoners both Italian and African stated they were completely demoralized when up against them in the thick bush of the boundary region. These cars were an excellent weapon for skirmishing round the water holes. They could charge through practically any of the bush spraying bullets all round. Had the enemy brought up anti-tank weapons the story might have been different but even so the highly mobile Armoured Car would have had the advantage in the thick bush with its very limited visibility. The cars were proof against all small arms fire and the Breda "Pillar Box" bomb did little more than scar the paint though it made a tremendous noise. These little bombs which were often used as warning signals could sometimes be plainly heard for five miles and at other times for only a few hundred yards. This discrepancy was very puzzling and was probably due to a combination of bush and atmospheric conditions.

Next day patrols were sent out in all directions but no important information was gained. Enemy casualties in the advance to Liboi turned out to be four killed and several wounded including a Bande Corporal who gave valuable information. On the 26th the bulk of the Battalion moved back to Liboi, leaving "A" Coy about 6 miles North East in the thick bush near the Lak Dera, and "C" Coy covering a water boring party at a point about $4\frac{1}{2}$ miles beyond the Boundary Cut on the Hawina road. It looked as if we had arrived at the limit of our advance, however on the 27th the C.O. Major Hurt who had taken over sometime previously from Major Herapath, was ordered by Brigade to stage a raid in force on Hawina. The C.O. managed to persuade the Brigadier to allow him to occupy Hawina instead of returning after the raid. At this point Lt. Col. J.R.H. Dowling arrived from Middle East to take over command but Major Hurt was directed to continue in command of the raiding force which comprised "B" and "D" Coys, 5, K.A.R., two platoons and one Detachment of Mortars from Headquarter Company, Two platoons S.A. Armoured Cars, a Reconnaissance party from the 1st S.A. Field Company all carried in three sections from 59 R.M.T. Company, with one platoon "B" Coy 1st. K.A.R. as escort for the transport. At 3 o'clock on the afternoon of the 28th the force set out from Liboi and lay up for the night on the edge of the thick bush eight miles short of Hawina. A Savioa of the Regia Aeronautica passed overhead during the move but did not appear to notice the column which was in pretty thick bush at the time. Just before reaching the bivuoac area three signal bombs were heard but no further sign of the enemy.

Next day the column advanced through thick bush, flanking the armoured cars which moved up the centre in bounds; almost immediately after the start another signal bomb was heard to explode and it was felt that the enemy would be well aware of the approach of the column·

Just short of the water hole at Hawina resistance was encountered in the form of Breda Bombs and rifle fire.

The Armoured Cars immediately went into action and "swept through the occupied area" while Mortar Fire directed by Capt. Hughes Young was brought down on the road East of the water hole. The infantry followed up the Cars in great style crossed the clearing and took up a defensive position East of the pan. At 08.45 hours the success signal was sent back to Brigade Headquarters and by 10.00 hours the Armoured Cars, which had patrolled four miles to the East, reported no enemy seen. A few minutes later an Army Co-operation Machine of the S.A. Air Force reported six Bande two miles East of Tabda but no enemy elsewhere. That afternoon on orders from Brigade one platoon of "D" Coy (Capt. Stopford) with two sections of armoured cars patrolled twelve miles down the road to Tabda where a few signal bombs were heard but no enemy seen. In the evening a patrol from "B" Coy under 2/Lt. Warton searching for a Bande camp South East of Hawina came upon a burning lorry. This, an enemy supply and ammunition vehicle, had been cut off by our advance and abandoned. The remaining enemy fired a few rounds wounding an askari and then disappeared into the bush.

The pan at Hawina was found to hold some 18,000 gallons of water, but Tabda was dry. It was estimated that Hawina Italian officers who had mostly fled at the approach of our had been garrisoned by a couple of hundred Bande under column.

5 K.A.R. had now liquidated the first two enemy posts on the road to Afmadu and it was the turn of another Battalion to take the lead, but first some important pieces of patrolling had to be done.

On 30 January 1941 an Armoured Car and Mechanised Infantry patrol under Capt. Hughes-Young reached a point two miles West of Beles Gugani, the next water of any importance which had been marked on a captured map as the enemy's next line of resistance. A few warning shots and bombs were heard but no further information gained. That afternoon the Brigade Intelligence Officer, Capt. Croskill, arrived carrying instructions that although it was the role of the 1st K.A.R. to make good Beles Gugani, 5 K.A.R. were required to obtain definite information as to its strength.

At this time the Regia Aeronautica were fairly active sending over their Caproni Bombers with some regularity. Our own air craft were based on an air field back at Haga-Dera and messages seldom reached them in time for them to take effective action. Later however the procedure was speeded up and some exciting air pursuits were seen. This activity by the Regia Aeronautica hampered mechanised patrol work and particularly interfered with a patrol from "D" Coy trying to find a route for a possible flank attack on Beles Gugani. A patrol under 2/Lt. Winnington-Ingram did much useful work and occupied the small water hole at Gheldezzo on the end of the "made road" (as opposed to the camel track) from Beles Gugani. At 05.45 Hrs. on February 1st Captain Hughes Young with a strong fighting patrol of three platoons "B" Coy, one Sec. Armoured Cars and a Detachment of Mortars, again left for Beles Gugani. This time they ran into strong opposition two miles west of the objective which was defended by Bande, and Colonial Infantry supported by Medium Machine Guns and Mortars. Having obtained the required information the patrol withdrew but an armoured car broke down and infantry had to be sent back to extricate it, costing us five casualties.

On the way back the column was ambushed in the thick bush, one lorry being destroyed and one man killed. The remainder ran the gauntlet and shot their way through. Enemy casualties were estimated at twelve killed.

On the morning of the 2nd February the 1st K.A.R. passed through the Battalion at Hawina and captured Beles-Gugani. The actions at Hawina and Liboi had broken the Bande operating on the 22nd Bde front. A few had been killed or captured, a few fell back on Beles Gugani, and some others to Abu Gala but most just drifted away back to their homes unwilling to face the "iron rhinos" any more. None deserted to us, perhaps because of the long standing feud with the Mohamed Zubir.

In connection with the engagements at Liboi and Hawina the following messages were received at Battalion Headquarters:

Telegram from H.Q. 22nd Bde, 3rd February, 1941. "Brigade Commander wishes all ranks to know that the G.O.C. E.A. Force has expressed his pleasure at the recent operations carried out by 5 K.A.R."

Letter from Brigade Major 22nd Bde to Major Hurt dated 5th February. "I am instructed to convey to you and all under your command in the operation at Hawina the Divisional Commanders congratulations on your neat and bold work which has resulted in the capture of very valuable information. Will you please see that all those under you are informed that their good work has been fully appreciated both by the Divisional and Brigade Commander."

The stage was now set for the capture of Afmadu which stands as a sentinel at the fork of the roads leading to Gelib and Kismayu. Set in a clearing in the bush, the village is built on slight rise in the ground and entirely surrounded with barbed wire five feet high and some yards thick. Preparations for its reductions started in earnest on the 10th when the Artillery and Mortars commenced ranging and intermittent shelling. On the evening of that day a heavy aerial attack was made, mostly by Junkers of the S.A. Air Force lasting for nearly two hours. This was the Battalions first and only real experience of heavy air attack and, though no doubt small in comparison to similar attacks in other theatres of war, concentrated on such a small target it was awe inspiring enough. At first light next morning the Artillery brought down concentrations and at 05.00 the 6th K.A.R. went in to the attack through gaps in the wire blown by the sappers. The result was some thing of an anti-climax for the fort was found unoccupied the defenders having evacuated during the night.

In this action the 5th K.A.R. had little to do save demonstrate against the wire, to draw away attention from the main assault, and help to soften up the defensive with fire from their mortars.

By six o'clock in the morning Afmadu was in our hands and the Brigade Commander following hard on the heels of the 6th K.A.R. entered and gave orders for the immediate pursuit of the enemy. At first this task fell to units of the 6th K.A.R. but they soon ran into trouble and in an ambush lost several men with others missing. "B" and "C" Companies of 5th K.A.R. were then ordered out to relieve 6th K.A.R. and carry on the pursuit. Hardly had they left on this task when the remainder of the Battalion was also ordered out on the same duty. After a little while the Company of the 6th K.A.R. was encountered having extricated themselves, and although they provided a guide the Battalion was unable to locate the site of the ambush, so dense was the bush. The decision was then made to continue on down a camel track leading in a South Easterly direction. Expecting an ambush at any moment the Battalion moved through the thick bush on a broad front. The day was extremely hot with a shade temperature early in the morning of 105 degrees Fahrenheit. By mid-day it must have been much in excess. The going was tough; underfoot was a sandy soil and the bush extremely thick with patches of sansovera every so often which pierced through clothing and puttees. Overhead flew a reconnaissance Aircraft of the South African Air Forces with which touch was kept by means of the T panel code. The information given was constantly negative, and it looked as if the enemy had made good their escape. By 3.30 in the afternoon when spirits and bodies were flagging from sheer exhaustion the Battalion came on a fork in the track with the marks of motor vehicles having moved down the right hand track. On went the Battalion now much cheered by this positive evidence of the enemy but shortly afterwards orders were received from Brigade, to leave one Company to investigate the track and find the enemy if possible, while the remainder of the Battalion was to return to Afmadu. The C.O. Major Hurt (Lt. Col. Dowling had been relieved of his command a few days previously) and "D" Coy pushed on down the track and eventually arrived at the deserted enemy camp after dark. There was found a great quantity of stores of all sorts, including food, ammunition, water containers, etc. Motor transport was brought up and the Company together with the more important items of enemy stores were brought in that night, arriving back at Afmadu a little before mid-night. Although the total march of the Battalion was only a matter of some 12 to 14 miles the troops were completely exhausted. due to a combination of lack of sleep for the last few days, the extreme heat of the day, and the very hard going. Of all the marches the Battalion undertook during the War, this comparatively short one ranked in conjunction with the training march to Shaffa Dinka. and the approach march to Palel in the Burma operations, as one of the most arduous.

Some criticism has been levelled at the Brigade Plan of attack in that the enemy were permitted to escape. Nevertheless the main objective was to clear away the last obstacle before the line of the Juba River and that very afternoon while the Battalion was wearily trudging through the bush two fresh brigades of the 12 Division were pouring through Afmadu on their way to the Juba. Had the enemy put up a stouter resistance, or had they been contained this movement must of necessity have been delayed. Judged from the defenses of Afmadu it is doubtful whether infantry unassisted by tanks could have reduced it, though in the end it must have fallen if surrounded due to shortage of water within the perimeter. It is of interest to note that the plan of defence seems to have followed fairly closely our own scheme for the defence of Wajir, in that comparatively few troops were in Afmadu itself the bulk lying up in the camp found six miles to the South East. But there it is to be hoped the similarity ended.

Although the Battalion did not know it the operation at Afmadu was to be the last planned operation in which they were to take part in Italian Somaliland. From Afmadu on, apart from some mopping up patrols in the Merca—Mogadiscio area, the Battalion tagged along as part of that great mechanised advance on Addis Ababa, until taking the lead from the South Africans in Dire Dawa they were called upon to force the crossing of the Auasc River the last barrier before Addis Ababa.

The day after the fall of Afmadu was spent by the Battalion in resting, washing, and inspecting the defences. The only notable event was the discovery of the wreckage of a crashed Anson Photographic Reconnaissance aircraft with the graves of the South African Airmen hard by.

On the 14th February orders were received to proceed in Motor Transport, at the unprecedented speed of 25 miles in the hour to a point 8 miles North of Kismayu.

In one swift movement of six and a half hours the column pushed down the road as yet undamaged by the passage of heavy vehicles. Passing through the 1st K.A.R. holding the cross roads of Saa Mogia, little knowing that a large mine field had been all around except on the road itself, the column entered a gap in the sand dunes and there before it lay the town of Kismayu with the blue Indian Ocean sparkling in the sun light beyond. For the best part of the last nine months the Battalion had been "bush whacking" and we felt then something of the same emotion which must have stirred Xenophon and his ten thousand as they caught their first glimpse of the sea four hundred years before the Birth of Christ. More prosaically we described it as "better than a bottle of Champagne".

The Armoured Cars had already proved the outer defenses to be unmanned and Brigadier Fowkes himself in an Armoured Car entered the town to establish its evacuation. Returning from this rash but gallant little jaunt he ordered 5 K.A.R. to make a formal entry at once.

"A" Coy were given the honour of leading the column. The Company Commander, still possibly suffering from the tonic effect of the sea, being quite unaware that the Armoured Cars and the Brigadier had already been into the town, thought that the advance was to be a tactical one, though perhaps rather rash and following the custom of such moves took his place in the third vehicle. From this he was summarily ejected and placed by the Brigadier in the leading truck with the valediction "off you go and I hope you don't get blown up" which of course was what he was himself fervently hoping. It was not till years after the war that he learnt the true state of affairs.

At 16.15 hours on the 14th February 1940 with "A" Coy's Union Jack flying from the leading vehicle the column entered Kismayu. One writer has described the streets as "lined several deep with the cheering populace" but this writer is prepared to swear that all he saw was a few miserable old Somali women croaking before the doors of their hovels, for the rest the town appeared to him as silent as the grave. Here and there were chalked inscriptions on the walls to the effect "We will return. Long live the Duce." The Duce is dead but after ten years the Italians have returned.

For the next two or three days the Battalion stayed in the Kismayu area carrying out patrols, including sailing by dhow to inspect the defences on the two islands in the bay. The Companies were mostly distributed around the perimeter "A" Coy going back to Saa Mogia to relieve the 1st K.A.R. on the cross roads.

On the 17th the Battalion concentrated and moved back again by M.T. to the Afmadu area leaving "C" Coy. at Kismayu. "A" Coy entering the town again by march route from the Saa Mogia cross roads were greeted by some South African troops with the rather irritating comment "You can come in now boys it's quite safe". "A" Company passed by on the other side.

Arrived in the Afmadu area the Battalion remained static until the 20th, during which time the 1st S.A. Brigade and the 24th Gold Coast Brigade were busy forcing the line of the Juba intent on the capture of Gobwen and Gelib. A further company, "B" Company was detached from the Battalion to garrison Afmadu and it looked as if the Battalion were to be rather back numbers when suddenly they were ordered to proceed at once to Bullo Erillo, about 50 miles to the East on the Juba River, to assist the 2nd Gold Coast Battalion whose task was in turn to assist the main operation against Gelib by capturing Alessandra from the North, "D" day being 22nd February.

Arrived at Bulo Erillo two platoons of "A" Coy proceeded on a reconnaissance, under orders of O.C. 2 G.C.R., of the river and the approaches to Alessandra. They reported the route suitable to M.T. with a little work and the villages clear of enemy though obviously only recently evacuated. This patrol though not particularly lengthy or difficult was notable for the excellent wireless inter-communication by No. 18 sets between the patrol and Battalion Headquarters who were kept in touch every quarter of an hour. Meanwhile the Battalion had been further dispersed with the despatch of "D" Coy to Mabungo a bridge head 25 miles further upstream where the 23 Nigerian Brigade were operating, and to which Headquarters of 24 Gold Coast Brigade were also moving.

On the 22nd as planned the Gold Coast Battalion left for their attack on Alessandra, what was left of 5 K.A.R. taking over their positions. The Gold Coast "B" Echelon Transport following up behind, perhaps too closely and without the certainty of a clear road, were ambushed by a Colonial Infantry Battalion withdrawing from their positions downstream. Several lorries were destroyed and a number of personnel killed and wounded. Just at this moment "C" Coy arrived unexpectedly from Kismayu. Although the noise of the battle was heard at Battalion Headquarters they had no information until the arrival of the G.S.O.2 Major Fisher at half past four in the afternoon. It was decided then that it was too late to take effective action but "C" Company should leave early the following morning to render any assistance they could to the Gold Coast; the remainder of the Battalion less "B" Coy were to proceed to Mabungo, "C" Company to follow on later, and to come under command of 11 (EA) Div.

Thus the Battalion did not take part in the stirring dash made by the remainder of the 22nd Bde which cut its way through the bush in the good old 1914—1918 style with the object of cutting off the retreat of the enemy from the Gelib and Gobwen positions. (The brigade under Brigadier Fowkes did reach their objective in time to capture many of the fleeing Italians but not before a large number of the early birds had already flown. Appreciating the situation the brigade turned North and set off in hot pursuit although indeed this role had been assigned to the Units of the 11th Division. 1 K.A.R. (Lt. Col. MacNab) in the lead cunningly keeping one jump ahead of any orders restraining his advance. On the 24th February the advanced elements of the Brigade reached Merca 150 miles North of Gelib and there they condescended to rest awhile.)

Meanwhile "D" Coy had been established at Mabungo for a few days and while they were placidly bathing in the river a sudden attack developed from the direction of Bardera on the Nigerian troops holding the bridge head. Headquarters 24 G.C. Brigade were at the time crossing over and without more ado, turned round their vehicles and recrossed with the utmost speed, "D" Coy covering the withdrawal. In actual fact this "counter attack" was probably accidental as it appeared later that it was delivered by forces from Bardera on their way to re-inforce Gelib, who unaware of the crossing at Mabungo, ran into the bridge head troops quite unexpectedly in the thick bush. Be that as it may they did not press home their attack and "D" Coy did not have to go into action.

With the fall of Gobwen and Gelib and the arrival of 11 Div. Headquarters at Mabungo the scene was set for the race to Mogadiscio. This was carried out in two Echelons. Echelon 1 being the fighting troops and Echelon 11 the soft core escorted by 5 K.A.R. less "B" Coy still at Afmadu, and "D" Coy in Echelon 1, all under the Command of O.C. 5 K.A.R., Lt. Col. Hurt.

The column moved in the rear of Echelon 1. Halting for the night was easy as the column merely went on until it bumped the rear of Echelon 1 and then parked down in the bush on either side of the road. Starting in the morning was another matter as Echelon 1 frequently did not know their own start time until the last moment, which complicated matters as there were some 15 separate units to be notified and over three hundred vehicles in the 2nd Echelon column. At first there was some little confusion in getting the column on the move in the right order and the control officers were kept busy but after the first day or so the units were past their start lines dead on time and there was little for the control to do except check them through.

The move commenced on the 23rd and that night the column halted north of Gelib, which was entered next day and turning North along an excellent road reached a point some fifty miles North of the town. Here the column was held up for some hours owing to traffic jams further North and did not leave till two o'clock the following afternoon. reaching Modun, just West of Brava, by nightfall. By now the bush country had given way to the more open country of the coastal belt with its sand dunes running down to the sea on the East. Next day, the 26th, the column reached Merca a day behind 22 Bde Headquarters and the 6th K.A.R. On reaching Merca the column split up in different directions and 5 K.A.R., picking up "D" Coy who had been dropped off by echelon 1 at Vittorio D'Africa, camped for the night on the sand dunes by the sea just South of the harbour.

With the arrival of the East African Forces in the Merca —Mogadiscion area the first stage of the Abyssinian campaign, the conquest of Italian Somaliland, was virtually complete.

Since leaving Garissa on the 23rd January the Battalion had come seven hundred miles in thirty three days of which about eight were not spent on the march. They had captured Liboi, and Hawina, and occupied Kismayu. They had assisted in the occupation of Afmadu, the passage of the Juba, and the capture of Gelib. From all these operations their causalties had been negligible. Two Europeans wounded, one African killed and five wounded.

The flag that was hoisted in Kismayu on the 14th February 1940 belongs rightfully to the 5th K.A.R. but all efforts to retrieve it have failed.

CHAPTER 5.

THE ADVANCE TO ADDIS ABEBA.

For three weeks the brigade remained in the Merca—Mogadiscio area, resting, refitting and mopping up, while the rest of the 11th Division were pouring North hard on the heels of the fleeing Italians.

5 K.A.R. soon moved from their sea side camp on the dunes and all officers and men were comfortably billetted in good quarters. "A" and "C" Coys were principally engaged on patrol work rounding up stragglers from the Italian Forces and bringing in arms and equipment while "D" Coy was charged with maintaining law and order and the recovery of household goods looted by the Somali from the farms which, on our advance, had been evacuated by the civil populace. After a short "reign of terror" the majority of looted goods were stacked by the Somalies outside their villages and brought into Merca. "A" and "C" Coys were equally successful in their missions and a steady stream of prisoners and equipment arrived at our Headquarters.

Meanwhile the lighter side of life by the seaside had not been neglected and regular bathing parties were organised for all ranks. Parties too set off to visit Mogadiscio, and in the evenings the local cafe at Merca was well patronised. The South African element in the garrison also seemed to be enjoying themselves but since their form of relaxation took the course of trying out captured enemy small arms in the "built up area" they were soon banished to the aerodrome where no doubt they repented themselves of the high spirits which had lost them a comfortable Mess. One never to be forgotten amenity of Merca was the wild fowling on the Webbi Shebelli near "A" and "C" Companies headquarters. There every sort of wild fowl common to East Africa abounded and more than once fifty brace fell to four guns in a couple of hours.

Merca then was a good place in which to relax a while after the strain of the previous few weeks. There was just enough work to keep the Battalion in trim and enough play to keep it happy, so it was with mixed feelings that it received its orders to continue the march northwards on March 21st.

The first few days were easy going along the excellent tarmac road from Mogadiscio to Ferfer built for the armies of Marshal Graziani. Along this road the column was able to average 22 m.p.h. in spite of the, by now, delapidated condition of the vehicles. Soon the road lead up into the hills and the last night stop on the tarmac at Belet Uen was comparatively cool. After Ferfer the road became worse and worse alternating between very rough metalling and loose sand, although, oddly enough, some isolated patches of tarmac had already been completed.

It must be explained here that the 22nd Bde were the last Bde in the 11th Division to proceed North following up behind the 23rd Nigerian Bde who were in the lead up to Harar and the 1st South African Bde who led from Harar to Miesso where the 22nd Bde took over from then.

At Lamma Bar the first night in Abyssinia, an unfortunate incident occurred. The driver of the Quarter Master's lorry set fire to his vehicle while attempting the fill his petrol tank with the aid of a naked lamp. The driver was himself immediately engulfed in flames and taking fright ran into the bush a fearful flaming figure dying the next day as a result of his terrible burns. His mate also sustained serious injury.

From Lamma Bar onwards the country gradually rises to the high plateau but the bush is still thick and it is extremely hot by day. At Gabredare the Battalion overtook Advance Force Headquarters and in the evening were honoured by a visit from the G.O.C. Lt. Gen. A. C. Cunningham, accompanied by Brigadier K. Edwards the B.G.S.

On the 26th March a swirling sandy desert where each vehicle chose its own route was crossed and then on through Sassabaneh, the scene of a Graziani battle, and Dagah Bur to camp in the savanah country 54 miles North. This was the first really cold night, some 4,500 feet above sea level. Next day the column came out on the open downlands round Giggiga, declared by some of the Battalion's Kenya farmers to be excellent grazing.

At Giggiga "A" Coy was dropped off to give local protection to Advanced Air Base and Advance Force H.Q. which arrived the same day. "A" Coy eventually rejoined the Battalion at the Auasc River but had quite an exciting time at Giggiga for on 29th March about nine Fiat fighters attacked and destroyed four of our planes on the ground before our Hurricanes could take off. When they did they shot down three of them for the loss of a fifth plane. On the 30th two Savoias came over and dropped bombs but caused no damage. They were chased and both shot down. On the 31st following a report of enemy some twelve miles away No. 5 Pl (2/Lt. Watson) gave chase and returned in triumph with 58 prisoners, 10 Camels and much equipment.

Meanwhile the remainder of 5 K.A.R. were pushing on over the formidable Marda Pass camping for the night of 27/28th March at Mile 22 on the road Giggiga—Harar, and nine miles further on the next night. Here the Battalion remained for three days clearing up the Nigerian's battle field in the Babile Gorge, and bringing in prisoners from the surrounding hills. On 31st March the Battalion again moved on, this time to camp on open ground just North of a large lake between Harar and Diredawa. It was very slow progress owing to traffic jams consequent on the occupation of Harar and it was dark and freezing cold before the last companies reached camp. The very last to arrive was Lt. Furse and his platoon which had been driving night and day all the way from Afmadu in a manful effort to catch up before all the fighting was over.

Descending Dire Dawa escarpment the next day along the edge of the precipice was a giddy affair. The demolitions made by the retreating enemy had only just been repaired by the South African Engineers and required careful navigation. (Later in the day a truck did turn over seriously injuring an askari). At Dire Dawa the road turned West along the railway line and after halting for a few hours at Urso orders were received to prepare to move forward again at 01.00 hours on the 2nd April, when 22 Bde were due to take the lead from the 1st S.A. Brigade which had run out of petrol at Miesso. The approach march may now be said to be over so it is convenient to pause for a moment and review the situation.

The Battalion had except for the few days at Babille, been constantly on the move for a fortnight. That no untoward occurrences hindered the smoothness of the operation must be put down to the excellence of the Brigade planning and the strict convoy discipline enforced. The start of a morning was fascinating to watch. Fifteen minutes before start time not a soul or a vehicle could be seen on the road, then would be heard the starting of engines and as the minutes ticked by an observer would just have been able to see general movement in the bush, the flash of a windscreen here or perhaps the dull gleam of a radiator cowling there. Precisely at the appointed hour the first vehicle would pull out onto the road to be followed by the next and the next in the schedule. Away down at the tail of the road might be seen the column of dust as another unit drove up the road to take its place in the order of march. In the evenings the same procedure but in reverse. The Reconnaissance party would have been ahead with marking flags and, as their unit arrived, the vehicles would turn off the road in succession and would be lead through their area, generally in a semi circle, each sub unit drawing off its own vehicles. The most criminal offence, which brought immediate retribution on the head of the offender, was for a vehicle to halt on the road thus holding up the smooth flow of the lengthy column. Breakdowns were of course numerous and in this event occupants were required to push their vehicle to the side of the road and await the arrival of the breakdown gangs which travelled at the rear of most units. Comparatively few vehicles had to be abandoned.

The drivers of the R.M.T. Coy lifting 5 K.A.R. were Cape Coloured boys with no experience. Recruited in the Union only a few months before, they were an enthusiastic and likeable lot (except when in liquor) but their driving was a nightmare, nevertheless they completed the trip with not more than the average number of accidents which was a most creditable performance.

Water was strictly rationed each vehicle carrying a forty gallon drum. At least one section Corporal (coloured) complained his drivers were a useless lot as they wasted water by washing their faces. Seeing that for most of the route the column moved in a thick swirl of dust this "wastage" was perhaps justifiable.

That we still had petrol enough to overtake the stranded South Africans was due entirely to the foresight and cunning of Brigadier Fowkes who busied himself at Mogadiscio by running (one hesitates to say smuggling) forward as much petrol as he could lay hands on and forming a dump from which we were able to refill our tanks and in addition take on a forty gallon drum per vehicle, some had two. This combined with the strictest petrol discipline enabled the Brigade to win the race to Addis. Each night the petrol tanks of every vehicle plus their reserves were measured and submitted to Headquarters who in turn submitted a consolidated petrol state to Brigade. Brigade would then, if necessary, make an adjustment as between units.

When the column did eventually roll into Addis Abeba it was with half full tanks, and as far as 5 K.A.R. were concerned they had but fifty miles of petrol left.

We were (at 1 o'clock in the morning of the 2nd April 1941) about to overtake the 1st S.A. Brigade at Miesso 170 miles from Addis, behind us lay the 23rd Nigerian Brigade and in front the formidable Auasc Gorge. For sometime we had heard of this position which was reputed to be very strong and as it was the last barrier before the Capital it was felt that here at all events the enemy would make a stand. Although the honour of being the first to assault this position was great we felt that it was an honour which we might, regretfully perhaps, have been prepared to forgo for some less hazardous task.

At one in the morning the Battalion set forth, driving without lights, along a good but winding road made difficult by the frequent demolition of bridges. As these were nearly all over dry or semi dry river beds they were negotiated without grave difficulty. By 11 o'clock we had come up to the enemy rearguard at Arba with which the 6th K.A.R. were successfully dealing. After a brief halt to allow them to complete their operation the Battalion passed through seeing several enemy corpses and guns on the side of the road and by 17.15 hours bivouaced down on a small ridge 2¼ miles East of the Auasc River.

The troops under command of 5 K.A.R. for the action at Auasc were as follows:

        One pl. "C" Coy 3rd K.A.R. (M.M.G.)

        One Sec. A. Tk. Bty.

        One Sec. 22 Mtn Bty R.A.

        One Sec. 54 Fd Coy R.E.

        One Sqd. (less one tp) E.A. Armd. Car Regt.

An Armoured Car patrol was immediately sent forward to gain what news they could of the enemy dispositions and while they were away a muffled roar at 17.30 hrs. told the Battalion that the enemy had blown the road bridge, (the railway bridge had been blown some time before) and the dust of enemy vehicles withdrawing from the West bank of the river could be seen.

The Auasc Gorge was not in fact anything like as formidable an obstacle as the Battalion had been led to suppose. It is in fact a gorge cut by the river in an otherwise flat plain and indeed there is no pronounced topographical feature other than the gorge itself which one encounters with some unexpectedness. The Gorge is some hundred or more feet deep and spanned by a road and rail bridge in close proximity one to the other. Both had been blown. The Auasc River flowing at the bottom of the Gorge is about thirty yards wide, and in flood would be a deep and fast flowing torrent but at this time of the year it was at a low level and fordable without difficulty.

Reconnaissance Patrols sent out at first light on the following morning the 3rd April were fired upon by Medium Machine guns from the enemy's left flank and although positions could be observed on his right they did not open fire. As a result of this information the Mountain Battery registered with accuracy on the enemy's left flank and at 07.30 hrs. "D" Coy were ordered to close up to the lip of the Gorge opposite the road bridge and if opportunity offered try and get across while "C" and "B" Coys were to try their hand further upstream beyond the enemy's apparent right flank. As all seemed quiet "D" Coy decided to have an immediate go at it and while Lt. Valentine's platoon was directed to engage the enemy's left in the area of the wrecked railway bridge, and if possible cross by that means. Lt. Langridge and his platoon set off cautiously down the side of the Gorge with the object of trying to cross by the remains of the road bridge. (The depth of the river was not known at this time), Lt. Howard's platoon covering them across. ("D" Coys fourth platoon under Lt. Ridley had not as yet returned from a patrol). Lt. Valentine was soon pinned down in the open near the Railway bridge by heavy automatic fire from the other bank but they gave as good as they got; Pte. Boiyo handling his light automatic with conspicuous gallantry was subsequently awarded an immediate Military Medal.

Meanwhile, to the surprise of all, Lt. Langridge and his Platoon made good their crossing near the bridge, though there was a nasty deep pool which gave some trouble, and started scrambling up the steep escarpment on the far side without an enemy interference. As soon as they were seen to be safely on their way Lt. Howard and his platoon were ordered to follow although this left "D" Coy with no reserve at all pending the arrival of Lt. Ridley who was expected back at any minute.

As soon as Lt. Langridge reached the top of the escarpment he came under intense enemy automatic and rifle fire, probably also coming in for some of the "overs" from Lt. Valentine's battle on his right. Without hesitation he rallied his men and charged the enemy posts defeating them each in detail. For this gallant action Lt. Langridge was awarded an immediate Military Cross and L/c Farah a Section Commander, the Military Medal. While this action was taking place on the heights above him Lt. Howard crossed the river with his platoon and was making his way upward to join in the melee when a hitherto silent enemy machine gun post about half way up the ascent woke up to what was happening and opened up. By this time a number of V.I.Ps. in their Red Hats had joined "D" Coy's observation post on the East bank of the gorge and in no time the lip of the Gorge resembled a field of poppies. Appreciating the situation Lt. Howard instantly changed direction and led his platoon straight at the enemy post while in true theatrical style his shouts of encouragement "Come on fourteen platoon" could be plainly heard across the Gorge. Away on the right the AntiTank gunners decided to join in and before anyone could stop them they opened the rapid fire in the general direction of the enemy post and to the grave danger of Lt. Howard and his men. Reaching the enemy position a good few yards ahead of his men Lt. Howard could be seen to lean over the sangar wall and despatch the gunners with his pistol; the remaining occupants of the post immediately surrendered. For this action Lt. Howard was awarded an immediate Military Cross.

This incident has been given in some detail as it is felt that seldom has a decoration been awarded under such dramatic and picturesque surroundings and in full view of the staff.

Immediately this incident was over the remainder of "D" Coy crossed by the same route, Lt. Ridley providentially arriving in the nick of time and Lt. Valentine evacuating his position on the right flank followed on. The position was now made secure and mopping up operations commenced. While "D" Coy were having their battle in the central sector, "C" Coy was working round the left and soon began crossing unopposed at the old Habbash ford half a mile upstream. "B" Coy followed on and came into position between "C" and "D" by mid-day. So ended the defence of the Auasc which from an enemy point of view turned out to be a complete flop. There remained however the enemy position in Auasc Village itself which held the guns covering the bridge and other enemy units. The enemy guns failed to have any effect being hopelessly inaccurate but they did threaten the Battalion transport which C.M.S. Kirotho of Headquarter Company very intelligently took it upon himself to move back out of the danger zone. For this action he was awarded the East Africa Force Badge.

That the enemy had some guns accurately ranged on the bridge is beyond dispute since at about mid-day they put down a salvo on the bridge itself much to the discomfort of "D" Coy and a party of Italian prisoners who had been collected there prior to their evacuation to the rear. It transpired later that these guns never opened because the Italian Commander had no idea of what was going on round his forward defences and gave no order. The one and only salvo they did fire was merely clearing the guns before withdrawal.

By the afternoon the 1 S.A. Field Bty (Maj. Rex Simpson) had arrived on the East Bank and supported by this unit together with the 22nd Mtn Bty (Major Leach) "B" Coy at 5 o'clock in the evening went in to clear up the village. After a brisk encounter the village was occupied and a rich haul of prisoners taken. Later that evening enemy vehicles were heard approaching and C.Q.M. Jarett left with a platoon to investigate. Before long they ran into trouble but beating off the enemy they returned with five prisoners but also with C.Q.M.S. Jarett severely wounded. He was evacuated that evening across the river but subsequently died of his wounds.

After the occupation of the village "B" Coy returned to their position between "C" and "D" Coys as it was thought possible that the enemy might make a counter attack. That he had some such intention is possible as during the night an enemy Armoured Car approached the positions but subsequently withdrew and no attack eventuated.

The following morning April 4th an inspection of the booty in Auasc was made. The village was indescribably dirty, smelly and fly ridden but there was the usual haul of guns and equipment. The positions there had been held by a hotch potch of troops amongst others, Savoy Grenadiers, Blackshirts, and Colonial Infantry. It is understood that the main enemy force was some miles down stream where because of the easier approach they expected the crossing to be made. They did not expect anyone to be so stupid as to try and cross at the road.

Meanwhile the 6th K.A.R. had come up and were hard at work improving the crossing above the bridge, both banks requiring attention before the wheeled vehicles could cross. By 2 o'clock in the afternoon a rough track had been made and the Armoured Cars were able to struggle across. Two hours later "B" Coy with as many armoured cars as had arrived set off in pursuit along the road to Addis.

Back at the road bridge the Sappers had been working frantically all through the night of the third of April and by the evening of the fourth it was open to traffic. Next morning the memorable race to Addis started. Capt. Buxton in the lead with "B" Coy encountered at 07.30 hours an Italian major and a party of Blackshirts who had been sent out with a request that the British troops enter Addis as soon as possible for fear of attacks by shiffta and disturbances within the town. By now the whole of 5 K.A.R. and attached troops were together again and the race to the Capital continued over grassy plains, up over the Mussolini pass with its peculiar volcanic formations and down again to Velencitte and Adama where a halt was made as here an important road leads away to the South. At intervals on the way curious phenomena were observed; notably car loads of War Correspondents who had been little in evidence up to now but had evidently come up for the big scoop, and Italian Motorcyclists, fierce G-men like figures in crash helmets mounted on powerful machines, presumably connected with the aforesaid Major. It was queer to see them racing alongside the Column when the day before they would have been shot, and, as yet, no Armistice. Still it was felt that as long as they were with us there was little risk of ambush. No doubt the Brigadier felt the same and he was obliged only to halt the column at Adama and Moggio to block the roads leading South and finally at Acachi where it was decreed the Brigade must halt to allow representatives of other formations to assemble before the ceremonial entry into the Capital the following morning.

At Adama the local population welcomed the column with enthusiasm but could give no information as to what enemy force lay to the South at Ponte Malcasa. A blocking force consisting of "B" and "C" Coys 5 K.A.R. with supporting arms all under command of the second in command 5 K.A.R. Major H. D. Tweedie were sent with all speed down the road to the river and there had an unexpectedly prolonged action at the Bridgehead, while the remainder of the Battalion were enjoying themselves at Addis. After an hour and a half's wait at Adama the column moved on up the escarpment through Moggio, where units of the 6th K.A.R. were dropped off to block the second road South, and so to Acachi four miles from Addis where a cold and uncomfortable night was spent.

Next morning the 6th of April 1941 the column formed up for the triumphal entry — first of all the War Correspondents were allowed to go on ahead: then a party consisting of "C" Sqn. E.A. Armd. Car Regts. Brigadier Fowkes and advance parties 1st S.A. Bde; then the South African Armoured Cars, General Weatherall and Brigadier Dan Pienaar Commanding 1 S.A. Bde; finally 22nd Bde Headquarters, 5 K.A.R. (less two Coys) one Coy 6 K.A.R. 22nd Indian Mtn Bty. Detachment 5 S.A. A/A Bty and one Platoon 3 K.A.R.

The entry to the Capital was made without incident. On the outskirts the column passed under a banner of welcome sponsored by the Greek community while the route through the town was lined with Italian Police and/or troops, who kept back the large but silent crowds. 5 K.A.R. drove straight to the aerodrome on the further edge of the town. There 1200 Airmen surrendered the following day marching up with their arms and equipment which they laid down in a dump. On the aerodrome too, were many burnt out or destroyed aircraft and many of the buildings were shot to pieces — a pity as we had to use them as temporary billets. The whole of Addis was completely surrounded with a thick belt of barbed wire as protection against attack by Shifta.

This perimeter was still manned by Italian Police and troops and so the Gilbertian situation arose that the conquering East African forces were billeted in a town guarded by their enemies.

5 K.A.R. were allotted the Aerodrome sector of the perimeter as their responsibility and various officers of the Battalion took over the more important posts spending the night in the Italian Officers' quarters. The Italians hourly expecting an attack by shifta were very "trigger happy". Whenever any noise was heard outside the perimeter they opened up on their fixed lines and so a considerable amount of shooting went on during the night for no apparent reason.

Everyone European and African alike were relieved that the long journey had now come to an end, proud that the Battalion and the 22nd Brigade had taken such a large share in the final stages and quite ready to settle down to a few weeks of garrison duty and revel in the luxuries of a captured town, as yet still flowing with wine and other good things brought in by the Fascists. The climate was pleasantly cool and apart from guard duties (at Divisional Headquarters, The Emperor's Palace, and other important places) and a certain amount of collecting of captured material all ranks had the opportunity of seeing the sights of this remarkable town. For good or ill however the Battalion only stayed three days before they were again off chasing General di Simone Southwards down the road to the Lakes. As a Unit the Battalion never returned to Addis though "D" Coy subsequently returned to carry out Prisoner of War Duties, and most British Ranks passed through at one time or another on their way to or from leave.

Originally it was intended, partly no doubt for Political reasons, that the 1st South African Brigade should complete the last stages of the advance and have the honour of entering the Capital first, and indeed much more publicity was given to their ceremonial entry a few days later, than to the entry of the 22nd Bde on Palm Sunday the 6th of April. Critical observers studying the numerous photographs of the entry of the South Africans will see amongst the crowd the faces of the Askari of the 22nd Bde.

But to give honour where honour is due the advance to Addis Abeba could not have been carried out so swiftly were it not for the sterling work of the South African Engineers and Road Construction Companies, not to mention the gallantry of the infantry in their many engagements with the enemy from Gobwen to Dire Dawa.

To be denied the final prize by so narrow a margin as a few gallons of petrol must indeed have been a bitter disappointment.

CHAPTER 6.

THE BATTLE OF THE LAKES.

On the morning of the 9th April, first Major Robertson Glasgow, Brigade Liaison Officer, and then Brigadier Fowkes himself arrived with orders for 5th K.A.R., and 2 Sec A.A. Bty to move down to Ponte Malcasa early the next day and continue the pursuit of the enemy forces which had withdrawn towards Sciasciamanna and the area generally known as "The Lakes". Meanwhile things had been happening at Ponte Malcasa and we must go back in time to April 5th to follow the fortunes of Major H. D. Tweedie's Force known as "Tweedcol" whom we left at Adama.

Tweedcol moved South from Adama at 14.00 hours on the 5th April. Almost immediately Major Tweedie's staff car broke down and delay was caused through having to transfer to the lorry following in the rear. Shortly after this one of our own aircraft swooped and dived bombed the rear lorry at the same time dropping leaflets in Amharic. This was not the first or last time that our columns were subjected to air attack by our own aircraft but on this occasion there was some small excuse as the lorry in question was a captured Italian vehicle. (Travelling in captured enemy vehicles was always a risky proceeding as not only did they excite our own air forces but also the murderous desires of the Shifta and Patriot Abyssinian forces). No serious damage resulted from this attack except to an Askari of "B" Coy who injured himself falling off the vehicle.

The distance from Adama to the bridge over the Auasc at Ponte Malcasa is about 12 miles. The leading Armoured Cars approached the bridge at 14.45 hours and received a hot reception from the South Bank. An Anti-Tank gun opened fire and knocked out the two leading cars. At the same time shelling from 65's, 75's and 105's came down on the bridge area and continued until dusk — chiefly air burst H.E. and shrapnel. The bridge itself had been completely demolished.

Soon "B" and "C" Coys were on the scene, "B" Coy with a detachment of the Battalion Mortars being ordered to secure the North Bank of the river while "C" Coy were deployed round the West flank fording the river where best they could and making good the Bridgehead.

A confused period followed with continued enemy shelling of the Northern approaches and some machine gun fire from both banks but by 15.30 hours "C" Coy had accomplished its task, capturing the Anti-Tank gun and its crew of three for the loss of two askari killed and three wounded. Meanwhile "B" Coy patrols cleared the North bank capturing one prisoner and being dive bombed again by our air force for their troubles.

By 15.45 hours the Nigerian Light Battery were in action shelling the road South of the bridge area where the enemy lorries could be heard moving. Some four miles South of the river the road ascends a steep escarpment. Concealed on this escarpment were the enemy 105's which out-ranged the light battery and continued shelling the bridge area with impunity. This state of affairs was rectified next day when the South Affican 60 pounders (said to have been taken off a World War I memorial in Johannesburg) arrived.

During the evening Colonel Hopkins Commanding the 2nd Nigerian Battalion came forward to take over the operations and at the same time came Capt. Henfrey with large numbers of Abyssinian Patriot Forces.

Throughout the evening the enemy transport could be heard moving South but after a cold and unpleasant night the enemy 105's opened again at first light in the morning. Little damage was done but a vehicle of the Nigerian Battery received a direct hit and went up in flames. By eight in the morning the Nigerians had taken over the bridgehead and all 5th K.A.R. troops were back on the North bank. Nothing very much happened that day which was spent in reconnaissance prior to the general attack planned for the following day. Early in the morning of the 7th the 60 pounders put down concentrations on the enemy positions and the Nigerians moved forward.

Tweedcol took no active part in this operation which was entirely successful and, after leaving "B" Coy to assist the East African Engineers under Major Gourlay to build a new bridge, moved back to garrison Adama. There they remained till they fell in with the Battalion on its arrival on the 10th.

Here again it is convenient to take stock of the general War situation in Abyssinia.

12th (African) Division were pushing slowly North from Neghelli, encountering bad weather and atrocious roads. On the 4th April they were at Uaddara about 30 miles North of Neghelli. Very little more was heard of them (from a Battalion point of view) until a Gold Coast Battalion arrived at Soddu at the end of May to take over from 5th K.A.R.

As for the 11th (African) Division, of which 5th K.A.R. formed part, the 23rd (Nigerian) Bde were garrisoning

Addis Abeba. The 1st South African Bde were chasing the enemy down the road to Gimma, and patrolling the hills around Addis Abeba collecting large numbers of prisoners from such places as Ficce and Debra Berhan. This Brigade was soon to be relieved by the depleted Nigerian Brigade (until strengthened by the arrival of 1st K.A.R.) and contained the enemy for many weeks at Abalti while the 22nd Bde were clearing up the Lakes area. Finally, early in June they attacked and captured the strong enemy positions on the Omo at Abalti at the same time as the 22nd Bde forced the crossing of the same river west of Soddu.

So much for the general situation.

On the 22nd Bde front (which with attached troops was known as Fowcol) the enemy appeared to be on the run. They had made no serious stand since the Juba and their morale was evidently at a low ebb. Their strategy seemed to be to withdraw fighting to behind the line of the Omo River into the Gimma area, where (presumably) a last stand would be made pending the expected help of German forces from the Middle East. Furthermore they were resolved to prevent the transfer of East African Forces to other theatres of War. Their forces now consisted practically entirely of remnants and it is not possible to refer to any one unit with accuracy. General di Simone from Somaliland commanded the force covering the 22nd Bde advance under the general direction of General Galimba, and his route after Auasc was Adama—Aselle—Bocoggi—Cofole (over a 10,200 ft. pass)—Sciasciamanna—Goluto—Soddu—Gimma. According to documents captured at Auasc he should have been at Sciasciamanna by the night of the 6—7th April but the rains were just starting and the road after Bocoggi was appalling, as we discovered later. His force included Blackshirt Battalions (CCNN), regular infantry (Fanterie) Blue Battalions (Airmen formed into infantry) Customs men (Guardia Finanza) Armed Police (Carabinieri) supported by 81 mm Mortars, medium and light tanks and a large amount of artillery, chiefly 65, 75 and 105 mms. At Gimma the enemy still had thirty bombers and six fighters which had escaped from Addis, while in the South opposing 12 (A) Division were the considerable remnants of at least three divisions.

The Duke of Aosta, the overall Commander, was reported to be at Agaro 20 miles North West of Gimma though he must have left shortly afterwards to organise the last stand at Amba Alargi.

Fowcol comprising the under-mentioned troops concentrated at Ponte Malcasa on the 10th April.

5th K.A.R.
6th K.A.R.
C Squadron 1 E.A. Armoured Car Regt.
1 S.A. Fd. Bty. (18 pounders)
18 Mountain Battery
22nd Mountain Battery
Sec 1 S.A. Med Bde (one 6" How One 60 lbs)
1 S.A.A. Tk. Bty.
54 E.A. Fd. Coy.
One Pl "C" Coy 1/3 KA.R. (Machine Guns)
1 (T) Fd. Ambulance

and on the morning of the 11th were off hot foot for Aselle with 5th K.A.R. in the lead. Starting at seven o'clock in the morning the force made good progress and soon had climbed up into the cold downland country around Aselle. At nine the head of the column reached a blown bridge near Gondi. On the near bank a large force of mounted Habbash were assembling while in the distance on the further bank could be seen a group of farm buildings, from which intermittent shots seemed to be coming. On investigation this was found to be Simba Farm, the centre of a large agricultural undertaking, containing much valuable machinery. Inside some hundred men, women and children had barricaded themselves against the attack of the Shifta. One attack had been beaten off the previous day but now the Shifta were massing for a final assault which the arrival of the British troops prevented. As it was, several of the inmates were wounded and the women hysterical with fear. In the centre of the farm yards was written in sacks a message to our air force. "Come and save us from the Abyssinians". Further up the road to Aselle the column came on an unpleasant sight. The last of the Italians trying to reach the farm had been ambushed, killed to a man, stripped naked and horribly mutilated after the fashion of the Habbash. In all twelve bodies were found.

At noon the column entered Aselle, a bitterly cold spot on the edge of the forest but with a fine view down to Lake Zuai. Here Fowcol halted and spent several days while the road South and the surrounding country was being reconnoitred. About 5 miles South of Aselle the road petered out though surprisingly enough again became metalled at about mile twelve. By now heavy rain was beginning to fall and it was obvious that the column would not succeed in forcing its way down the road under the prevailing conditions. "A" Company did, however, succeed in getting as far as Bocoggi where the Italian Residente and other local Italians had not yet been murdered. Other patrols in and around Aselle came on more civilian corpses including those of a Frenchman and a Pole. The local chieftain Fitarauri Okay was summoned to account for these atrocities but denied all knowledge though he promised to return the stolen cattle. This summons from the Brigadier was re-inforced by a demonstration of fire power from all arms of the brigade. Suitably impressed the Fitarauri fulfilled his promise and the troops had their ration of fresh meat.

Altogether Fowcol remained ten days in the Asselle area trying to find a way forward by repairing the road but in the end it was decided the Bocoggi route was impracticable for so large a force and orders were received to return to Adama and thence down the Moggio—Soddu road. Accordingly "Tweeforce" was again reconstituted of "A" and "B" Companies with two detachments of Mortars and one Platoon of Machine Guns under the Command of Capt. Tweedie and were detailed to garrison Bocoggi and demonstrate as far forward as possible to give the impression that they were but the van of a larger force behind.

On the 24th April the 5th K.A.R., less "Tweeforce" left Aselle for Bole Bridge via Adama and Moggio whither the majority of Fowcol had already proceeded. There the Battalion was set to work repairing the bridge, those not actively engaged in this work found the duck shooting much to their liking and reminiscent of Merca, over one hundred geese and duck being bagged. Heavy rain caused a rise in the river and the Battalion was still working on the bridge up to the 26th. On this day the Battalion was still more than ever depleted by the despatch of "D" Company to Buttagero, some twenty miles to the West which was thought might still hold some enemy forces. Two singular incidents befell this patrol. First having reached their chosen forming up place for the final phase of the patrol, out of the mists of the early morning thundered a troop of Abyssinian Horse, apparently bent on the destruction of the village. On encountering "D" Company the horsemen pulled up and it was found that a large percentage were in fact Amazons armed complete with lance and shield. As "D" Company were by now on foot it seemed as if the unfortunate Italians were in for a bad time as there was no restraining this band who galloped off into the mists ahead. The Company pressed on dropping off Lt. Howard and his platoon to bring up the transport as opportunity offered and with the rather vague instructions (there was no inter company wireless) that if he heard the "devil of a battle" to park the transport under a small guard and come forward at once.

In due course Lt. Howard heard the sounds of battle somewhat to a flank and true to his orders dashed into the affray to find himself involved in a battle between our erst-while horsemen and women of the early morning and a neighbouring tribe. (It was learnt later that this was the conventional Tournament Season in those parts during which the rival factions settled old scores). Meanwhile the rest of the Company had entered Buttagero unopposed and hearing the sounds of strife, and seeing no signs of Lt. Howard or the transport began to think the worst had happened. However, by the evening Lt. Howard turned up safely and shortly afterwards a large Band of Patriots under an Abyssinian Officer. British and Abyssinian flags were run up on an improvised flag staff and cups of tea handed round. Shortly after this the second singular incident of the day took place. "D" Company Officers had occupied the old Residente's house, a wooden structure which had been stripped of all its siding leaving the floor and roof intact supported by a number of pillars. Just at dusk a tremendous thunderstorm came up and a sudden gust of wind blew the whole frail edifice down, pinning the officers between ceiling and floor. As luck would have it they had already off loaded the lorries and spread various boxes around which saved them from being squashed flat and the worst that happened were a few bruises. The gale also blew down the flagstaff which was treated by the Habbash as being a very bad omen. After carying out patrols North and South without contacting the enemy the Company returned to join the Battalion which had by now moved on down the road to the Cross Roads, eight miles South of Adamitullo.

A few miles South of the Cross Roads the 6th K.A.R. had taken up a defensive position between Lakes Algato and Languna blocking the other approach to Sciasciamanna. Patrols sent out by the 6th K.A.R. round the Western shores of Lake Algato located an enemy position in some strength on Mount Fike (Italian Monte Fiche) a promontory South of the lake commanding the road to Sciasciamanna.

At dawn on 28th April two platoon "C" Coy under Capt. Kemble with the Intelligence Officer left to reconnoitre the Fike position making a wide detour through the thorn scrub to the West, and almost immediately found their vehicles stuck in the mud or in holes concealed by the long grass. By noon two section had managed to get as far as the River Gidu which flows into the lake from the West and having struggled across found themselves involved in a swamp, while behind them a large body of the enemy with mules were observed moving towards the river. Instead of opening fire on the patrol the enemy quietly gave themselves up, though one or two stouter hearted made good their escape. Attempts to follow up the escapees were made but soon the patrol found themselves in a thick bush with swamp land underfoot. Meanwhile reports had been sent back by runner and Brigade ordered 5th K.A.R. to move forward to the West of Fike and cut off the enemy's withdrawal to Soddu.

Accordingly at 16.30 hours the Battalion with the support of 1 S.A. Fd. Battery moved forward and camped for the night on the high ground where "C" Company had left their transport, and here at 2 a.m. next morning "D" Company rejoined them. Now that O.C. 5th K.A.R. had two rifle companies he asked and obtained permission to attack the Fike position instead of merely containing it. Early on the morning of the 29th "C" and "D" Companies with the Bty. O.P. set out on foot to the attack choosing as their crossing place a spot where smoke had been seen rising the previous day. Owing to heavy rain during the night the low lying ground was under water but not too treacherous and at 6 o'clock they reached the thick bush on the bank of the river. There they surprised a party of the enemy with two diesel lorries more or less bogged down and after a quick scuffle took them prisoners.

Just as O.C. 5th K.A.R. was re-organising for the next stage of the advance an urgent message was received from Brigade calling the attack off and ordering the Battalion back to the cross roads to guard against an imminent attack by an Italian Armoured column.

Warning of this attack had been relayed to Fowcol by Force Headquarters who had intercepted enemy wireless communications ordering General Bertello with an armoured force to move forward from Sciasciamanna and cut the East Africa Force Lines of Communication at Moggio. In fact this force did move a few miles up the road, had a look at the 6th K.A.R. positions and thought better of their adventure.

Back then the Battalion went to their old positions around the cross roads now somewhat expanded to fit "D" Company into the perimeter. That day and the next was spent in further reconnaissance of the Fike position but this time by a more direct route. The C.O. received orders to carry out his attack on Fike on the 1st May provided air reconnaissance had given the all clear as far as Bertello's Armoured Column was concerned by 08.30 that morning.

The Fike position was not in itself a naturally strong one but it had the advantage of a good all round field of fire except to the West where it was dominated by high ground covered with thorn scrub. The difficulty lay in trying to approach unobserved owing to its position between the two Lake Algato and Sciala and the flooded area on either side of the River Gidu which bifurcates a little short of Mount Fike, one arm flowing into Lake Algato, the other into Lake Sciala. It was accepted therefore that surprise could not be obtained, as to the intention to attack, and the river line, which was under observation from the enemy, would have to be crossed probably under artillery fire. Once across that obstacle it was expected that some tactical surprise could be obtained by attacking down hill from the high ground West of the position.

At 09.15 Brigade telephoned through the O.K. to start and the Battalion already embussed moved off down the track to the River line. Hardly had the advance started when two Fiat fighter aircraft came over, had a good look at the column from about one hundred feet, and flew off again without firing a shot. This was an ill omen with which to start an attack but in fact it made little difference for as soon as the column came out into the open plains the enemy guns at Fike opened fire, but fell a quarter of a mile short. Here the column debussed and deploying made its way down to the ford. Owing to the terrain the actual banks of the river could not be seen from the enemy position but they had it well ranged. However, rather as at Auasc they were too clever and instead of shelling the ford itself, they shelled the river on either side with some intensity. It was therefore possible to cut brushwood to lay in the ford and a section of 18 Mtn. Bty and the vehicles carrying the mortars and ammunition were safely got across though not without difficulty.

By two o'clock in the afternoon all troops were across and ready for the final advance. The Mountain Battery was in action 500 yards West of the ford and had registered accurately on the enemy positions.

Leaving one platoon of "D" Company to guard the guns Battalion Headquarters with "D" Company set off straight up the sloping ground towards the enemy position while "C" Company were sent round the right to gain the high ground as planned. Almost immediately "D" Company ran into light shelling but it is doubtful if it could have been observed fire as much of it fell behind the advancing troops, which in fact did more to speed the advance than anything else. A little later the enemy shortened their range and for a few minutes the position was uncomfortable but the advance continued steadily until the crest of the hill was reached about a thousand yards from the enemy, and in plain view. The shallow valley between, except for a small finger of thorn scrub on the left, was completely bare. For some unknown reason the appearance of "D" Company on top of the ridge facing the enemy seemed to be the signal for the enemy guns to cease fire and their gunners could be seen strolling nonchalantly about the position. It was thought that perhaps they had decided to call it a day but not a bit of it, for just as "D" Company started moving down the forward slope a murderous small arms fire was opened on them which forced them to ground. But again the enemy had misjudged things for they were obviously firing on fixed lines at the top of the crest and the bullets passed harmlessly over the heads of the prone company which replied with vigour. Unluckily, just at this moment the C.O. and his Adjutant Capt. W. D. Draffan reached the crest and Capt. Draffan received a bullet wound in the stomach. (Most fortunately and largely due to the skill of the Medical Officer, Capt. Kisner he completely recovered from this wound). The position was now, as far as "D" Company were concerned one of stalemate. Being widely deployed on a forward slope it was impossible to get any messages through to the platoons or the sections on the right and each time a section opened on the enemy, the enemy replied with gusto. However, Lt. Valentine's platoon on the left was in partial cover and O.C. "D" Company collecting as many men as he could, moved over to join Lt. Valentine and started a forward movement through the small amount of cover provided by the light bush on that flank.

Meanwhile "C" Company away on the right had reached their objective above the enemy position but were themselves faced with a bare open patch covered by the enemy's left flank defences. They had not been observed. The timing of the arrival of "C" and "D" Companies on their respective objectives was probably a matter more of good luck than anything else for as O.C. "C" Coy was wondering how to get across the open stretch on the enemy's flank, "D" Coy arrived on their front and as "C" reported later every enemy's head turned to look at "D" Coy and indeed some scrambled out of their trenches to re-inforce that front. Seizing this God given opportunity "C" Coy emerged from their cover and were more than half way across the clearing before they were spotted. By then it was too late to stop them and going in with the bayonet they rolled the whole position up. As soon as the noise of "C" Coy's attack was heard "D" Coy doubled down the forward slope but encountered no opposition and the action was over within a few minutes.

While "D" Coy were pinned down on their forward slope the Battalion Mortars under Capt. Trent had come into action with great accuracy and at least one direct hit was found on the enemy heavy machine gun position which had killed the crew and put the gun out of action.

The tale of the action at Fike would not be complete without reference to the stretcher bearer of "C" Coy who joining in their charge got his man by knocking him on the head with his stretcher and, and having laid him out, opened up the stretcher and calmly carried him off the field of battle. The enemy casualties in this brisk action amounted to twelve Europeans killed, twelve seriously wounded and sixty-three captured. Twenty seven native askari were killed, ten seriously wounded and ninety-three captured. The Battalion's casualties were one officer wounded, one askari died of wounds and two others wounded. An undated parade state found on the position gave the strength as eighty-nine Europeans and eight hundred and fifteen natives. Thus while nearly all the Europeans were either killed or captured, a large number of the natives must have deserted before the action though quite a number did make good their escape during it. Three 65 mm guns, two 20 mm AA/A/tk guns, eleven heavy machine guns, sixteen light Automatics and one hundred and fifty rifles together with ammunition and other stores were taken. This action shows the value of a simple, well timed and well executed plan. The enemy had again chosen a rocky knoll for a defensive position very vulnerable to Artillery or Mortar fire and made more so by their failure to dig good weapon pits, most of the fire positions being stone sangars.

That evening the transport came up and the wounded were taken away. Next day "D" Coy were sent back to clear up the mess and bury the dead while the remainder of the Battalion held the fort at the Adamitullo cross roads, General Bertello again threatening great things.

The Italians seemingly attached great importance to their position at Fike regarding it as the key to the defence of the Lakes covering as it did the approaches to Sciasciamanna. The G.O.C. 11(A) Division himself had paid considerable attention to its elimination and was good enough to send the Battalion a congratulatory message on the first anniversary May 1st 1942. A few days after the action Major Hurt received news of his promotion to Lt. Col. and confirmation of his command and very shortly afterwards was awarded the D.S.O. chiefly for his conduct of this operation.

For close on a week the Battalion remained in the Adamitullo area expecting the armoured attack that never came. Meanwhile patrols were sent forward along the track to Bubissa preparatory to the next stage of the advance. This came on the 6th May when the Battalion was ordered to form a bridgehead over the Gidu to allow the 1st Natal Mounted Rifles to pass through and capture Lokole, an occupied position some three miles beyond the river. The bridgehead was established against slight opposition though the forward troops had an anxious time in fording the river "which ought to be only three or four feet deep" against light automatic fire. And so it was but a few hours later it had risen several feet. This was a characteristic of the Gidu which rose and fell very quickly with the incidence of rain. The attack by the Natal Mounted Rifles was not very successful until the arrival of some light tanks, which with great difficulty, were man-handled across the ford. These tanks quickly dispersed the opposition which had been holding up the attack. The Natal Mounted Rifles were then withdrawn and after a day or two 5th K.A.R. were ordered to resume the advance directed on Bubissa. (The main Fowcol advance was down the direct road to Sciasciamanna and 5th K.A.R. operations towards Bubissa were designed partly as a blocking movement and partly as a holding operation to prevent reinforcements moving to Sciasciamanna). After a considerable amount of work on the ford it was made just passable to transport and the whole Battalion (Less "A" Coy), "B" Coy having rejoined on the 4th May arrived at Lokole on the 9th, the locals reporting enemy positions at Bubissa some six miles ahead, with guns and tanks. The next day the Battalion and its supporting arms of Mountain Battery, Armoured Cars and Engineer Detachments moved forward some miles to a small ridge, three miles short of the enemy and spent the rest of the day in reconnaissance. Owing to the rains all low lying ground was very soft and in places more or less of a bog which made the movement of wheeled traffic difficult. A general situation report was made as usual to the Brigade and that evening the following message was received." While I wish you to carry out your nuisance role as far as possible do NOT get heavily involved or badly stuck in the mud. Suggest you recce passage over your bog and confine operations to beating up enemy advance positions, until you hear from me again." Next morning, therefore, the 11th May, "B" Coy with two platoons from "D" Coy and supported by the 18th Mountain Battery, set off on a left flank movement "to beat up the enemy". Round the right flank went a small tank hunting party consisting of the one and only anti-tank gun (a captured weapon) in a lorry, three armoured cars and a posse of askari armed with anti-tank rifles (all under Command of O.C. "D" Coy who had a bad leg and couldn't walk). "B" Coy's attack went in at dawn as planned and was a complete success until the enemy woke up to what was happening and called up their tanks. Thereafter the enemy had it more or less all their own way. Meanwhile the tank hunting party was still a mile away, having had to push the lorry and the armoured cars a large part of the distance. One car was so firmly imbedded in the mud that it had to be abandoned. They were therefore unable to influence the battle and returned without firing a shot but picking up a number of Italians who had run away at "B" Coy's first attack. In an effort to assist "B" Coy a section of armoured cars was sent forward to draw off the tanks but unfortunately two of them became bogged and had to be abandoned. The situation was now rather serious and the Battery prepared to fire at the tanks over open sights but the tanks did not follow up their initial success and eventually withdrew, permitting "B" Coy to extricate themselves without serious casualties. From a nuisance point of view the operation was successful and some eleven Italian and eight native troops were brought in as prisoners but it must be admitted that on this occasion the enemy did succeed in "seeing off" the 5th K.A.R. The Battalion casualties were one officer missing, believed killed, two askari killed and eight wounded, while three armoured cars were abandoned. (All three were subsequently recovered though two had been stripped of equipment by the enemy). The missing officer was found alive and well at Gimma where he had been able to do some valuable shopping on "tick" promising to pay when the Battalion occupied the town. This arrangement entirely suited the local shop-keepers. Reports indicated that the enemy had about fifty killed and many wounded in "B" Coy's first assault, the garrison consisting of about eight hundred mixed European and African troops with seven medium and three light tanks supported by two batteries of artillery. If it had not been for the tanks which could manoeuvre on the soft ground which the armoured cars could not, it is certain that "B" Coy would have gained the day despite the heavy odds against them.

The problem of the tanks was difficult as apart from the one captured Italian anti-tank gun there was no weapon capable of dealing with the mediums, and so during the next few days while the Battalion was ordered "to hold a defensive position" and "attack as opportunity offers" various devices such as petrol bombs were thought up by the Engineers and plans laid for a night attack. This however was not to be for on the 13th orders were received "wish you withdraw behind Gidu as unobtrusively as possible. If you can stage a demonstration in front of enemy in morning so much the better. If Gidu impassable get back when you can can, you have fulfilled your role manfully." Accordingly "A" Coy who had rejoined the battalion on the afternoon of the Bubissa action staged a demonstration but reported very slight enemy activity. On withdrawing back behind the Gidu "D" Coy and a platoon of Machine Guns were left on the South bank as a bridgehead party. Next morning when the whole of the Battalion was ordered back to firmer (and drier) ground the river was found to be impassable,.one "D" Coy askari nearly being drowned in a gallant attempt to get a rope across. Before long the river was down sufficiently to enable them to cross and that evening the Battalion found itself concentrated once again on its old stamping ground at the Adamitullo Cross Roads.

It was therefore with a certain amount of irritation that it learnt two days later that it must return to the Gidu and make its way on foot (we had become rather lorry conscious by then) to Goluto, liquidating Bubissa "en route", where it would rejoin Fowcol main body which had just captured Sciasciamanna. Meanwhile the transport would travel by road to the same destination.

Back to the river then went the Battalion, less "B" Coy who escorted the transport, on the 17th only to find it so high as to be impassable. It fell during the night and by 7.45 next morning all were across and the march continued. Rather alarmingly an Abyssinian Chief reported that the Italians had re-inforced Bubissa but later on locals said it had been evacuated, which was subsequently confirmed by patrols from "A" Coy. A wet, cold and unpleasant night was spent on the Bubissa Ridge just behind the old enemy positions and in the distance towards Goluto could be heard the sounds of battle.

Next day the Battalion marched on and reached Goluto in time to see the Brigade Artillery shelling enemy transport withdrawing from the further bank of the Billate River.

The Battalion now came into Brigade Reserve and with them shared the unpleasant attentions of a flight of Fairey Battles which had been called up to bomb the withdrawing enemy but preferred the stationary brigade group. The Battalion did not receive any casualties from this unfortunate incident though other units suffered severely all the more because as by now there was no Air Threat from the Regia Aeronautica, the normal air raid precautions had fallen into abeyance.

The Battalion did not take part in the operations at Goluto which were undertaken by the 6th K.A.R. It was here that Sgt. Nigel Leakey of that Battalion gained a posthumous Victoria Cross for his gallantry in a single handed attack on the enemy's medium tanks.

The next two days were spent in mopping up and burying mutilated Italians found in the bush and on the 21st, the bridge over the Billate having been repaired, the Battalion again moved forward eventually reaching Soddu without further action, at dawn on the 23rd after a slow and miserable trip through rain and mud.

Here the forward elements of Fowcol, the 2nd Bn. Nigerian Regiment, had taken a rich haul of prisoners amounting to some three thousand officers and men including General Liberati, a charming white haired old gentleman (subsequently to die on the beaches of Berbera) commander of the Italian 25th Division responsible for the Sciasciamanna-Goluto-Bubissa sector. There too was General Baccari, Commanding the 101st Division, and Col. Ameria from Bubissa. Di Simone, Bertello and others had already made off towards Gimma. Seven medium tanks, probably those from Bubissa and large quantities of other war material was also taken.

Soddu was the key to the defence of Abyssinia South of Addis Abeba. Through it must pass the enemy withdrawing both from Fowcol's advance and the advance of the 12th (A) Division working up from Neghelli. Fowcol had, as it were, won the race to this important road junction and therefore it behoved them to make it secure against the remnants of the Divisions being pushed back by the 12th (A) Division. This task was allotted to the 5th K.A.R. The prisoners were herded in a camp in the open more or less in the middle of the town with "C" Coy providing the guards. "A" and "B" Companies were sent off to block the road leading up from the South and "D" Company held in reserve. Soon there was a foretaste of what was to come for on the day of establishing the road block a party of 37 Italians and 500 native troops marched up the road blissfully ignorant that the town had fallen, and being appraised of the fact quietly surrendered. During the next few days thousands of weary, footsore, hungry Italians and Africans toiled up the road from the South and were taken prisoners. They included General Gaffarati and most of his 21st Division from Giabassire. Some rode but most walked carrying all they possessed. One day a note from without the town addressed to the Residente enquiring how to deal with the enemy, was intercepted. A polite note was sent in return inviting them to join the others.

Only the 24th Division under General Pialorsi showed any initiative. They decided to skirt the town and strike across country to the Omo River and so to Gimma. But they fared little better for those who were not cut down by Shifta fell into the hands of Lt. Evans on patrol along the Abba-Kella road.

On May 27th the 3rd Gold Coast Battalion reached Soddu, after weeks of hard campaigning. (Running out of petrol they had to march the last stretches), and took over the defence of the town. 5th K.A.R. then concentrated on the "A" & "B" companies' positions just outside the town. Prisoners continued to stream in, mostly from the 21st Division. The more senior officers were sent straight back by lorry, but thousands of junior officers and men had to be herded together on the open moorland with only a single strand of wire as a fence. They had a pretty miserable time as the weather was cold and wet and the only protection they had was whatever they had brought with them, but no doubt it was better than the weary marching they had been doing for so long. Occasionally a Caproni bomber could be seen apparently dropping supplies to the remnants of the 24th Division struggling through the bush to the Omo and once or twice Fiat fighters flew over the town. After Soddu the Battalion never again saw an Italian aircraft in the air.

By 10 o'clock on the 28th May 9,000 prisoners had been collected mostly from units of the 21, 24, 25 and 101 Divisions.

Among other interesting prisoners was "Twinkletoes" — Major Bernadetti — the gallant commander of the Bande Group on the Italian Somaliland Border in the early days of the campaign; The Colonel in command of the Italian troops which had captured Moyale in 1940 (He said he had been ordered to go on to Marsabit but he couldn't because of the lack of supplies and the bad roads); The Residente of Italian Moyale and some Italian missionaries from Meru.

On the 29th, 5th K.A.R. (less B & D Coys left behind to assist in the garrison of Soddu) joined the Brigade column on the march to the River Omo and the final objective Gimma.

Progress was slow owing to the heavy rain and the congested roads. The forward troops had struck frequent minefields and it was unwise to leave the road without careful reconnaissance. The country between Soddu and the Omo is some of the most beautiful, fertile, and densely populated of any in Abyssinia. It is green and rolling with plenty of water but not of course conductive to fast progress during the rains. No movement was allowed on 30th May and it was not till late in the evening of the 31st that the Battalion reached camp at top of the escarpment overlooking the huge gorge of the River Omo Bottego. Here the Nigerians had caught a party of Italians before they made good the crossing of the river but had not escaped scot free themselves, receiving several casualties including one officer killed. Meanwhile working parties were repairing the road over demolition blown in it where it descended the escarpment to the valley below. Mines had been freely laid and caused a number of casualties to these parties.

The country was on a tremendous scale. Sensational as was the eastern side of the escarpment it was completely dwarfed by the western or far side which rose sweep upon sweep 6,000 feet above the valley floor, to the mountainous region of Mai Gudo over which lay the road to Gimma. The river itself was broad and swift and no bridge had as yet been completed, the Italians using a cable operated ferry. After a day or two spent in patrolling and getting the guns into position the plan of attack was ready and on 2nd June 5th K.A.R. were ordered to cross during the night preparatory to a wide encircling movement. The crossing was made in assault boats manned by the Nigerians who had several experienced watermen in their ranks. But the site chosen was not satisfactory and boat after boat was swept away by the current, several being swamped so that in the end only "A" Company managed to get across and the operation was suspended until a better crossing place could be found. Meanwhile the enemy had found the range and several salvos of shells came down causing casualties but not severe. "A" Company marooned on the far Bank during the 3rd had a brisk encounter with an Italian patrol which came down to investigate. After killing a number and capturing more, the patrol was driven off, having wounded Cpl. Khada who subsequently died of his wounds.

By that night a new and better crossing had been located and moreover one which did not appear to be under enemy observation. The assault boats were now giving trouble and one by one they had to be withdrawn for repairs. By midnight the rest of the Battalion was across (Less "B" Coy still back at Soddu) "D" Coy coming up in time to join in the fun. Not that the crossing was particularly enjoyed by anyone as the current was strong and the boats had great difficulty in making the other bank without being swept far down stream. The Battalion lay up in the long grass for the rest of the night being a bit disturbed by Hippos walking along the bank and through their ranks. Next morning June 5th, at first light, the encircling movement started lead by "C" Coy. The objective was the enemy 105 mm Gun positions, thereafter cutting the road behind what was believed to be the main enemy infantry positions.

The going was hard, up and down the gullies that ran down from the main massif : By noon the Battalion was up above the position of the 75 mm guns and sweeping down on them found them abandoned except for one wounded native and a couple of Italian gunners who were asking to be put in the bag. After a brief halt at this position the force again moved on signalling its position to our gunners on the Eastern Bank by flashing mirrors. Even so several of our own shells dropped unpleasantly close. By 5 p.m. after a march of ten hours or more and feeling a bit weary the Battalion arrived above the 105's position. The guns were in position but there seemed to be few gunners in the vicinity. Nevertheless "A" and "C" Companies formed up, with "D" Coy in reserve and swept through the position without opposition and turning slightly right handed made for the road. Before reaching it they ran into considerable opposition and in the gathering dusk a regular soldiers battle ensued. A counter attack lead by Capt. Della Noce, later to become the Battalion Interpreter at Gimma, gave "D" Coy holding the firm base some shooting practice, the mortars also going into action. This was gratifying for the mortar numbers who had all day been humping the bombs on their backs against just such an eventuality. After a brisk fight the counter attack fizzled out but the Battalion were in something of a predicament being surrounded on three sides, or so it seemed, by masses of the enemy, and as it was rapidly getting dark it was decided to withdraw a little to a better position, leaving a party to guard the captured guns. "A" and "C" Companies disengaged themselves but not entirely as a large number of the enemy insisted on being taken prisoners and returned with them to the bivouac area.

Meanwhile the Nigerians had also crossed the river and advancing up the road attacked frontally the position which the Battalion attacked on the flank. Early next morning explosions were heard high up the road and as expected this proved to be two large demolitions. The timing of these demolitions was very unsatisfactory for the Italian rear parties, three at least of their lorries beingh caught and blown up in the demolition. This action, the last before Gimma resulted in a bag of two thousand more prisoners as well as guns and general equipment. Next day work parties were sent up to the site of the demolitions and repair work started — made more difficult by the wrecked lorries. The remainder of the Battalion remained down by the river getting their transport across preparatory to resuming the advance to Gimma as soon as the road was open. Working night and day the extensive demolitions were repaired in record time and by 4'clock on the afternoon the head of Fowcol was approaching the cross roads at the Piccolo Gibbie bridge where it was known that Italian representatives would be waiting "with an important message." Excitement now ran high for Fowcol had learnt that the 23rd Nigerian Brigade, which had been waiting so patiently at Abalti had also forced the crossing of the Omo and were racing on Gimma from the North East.

Who then would reach the Italian emissaries first and receive the surrender of General Gazzera, the commander of all troops in South West Abyssinia? In the event our old comrades the 1st K.A.R., now part of the 23rd Brigade, beat us to it by a few minutes. The result was however something of an anti-climax as the Italian representatives were there merely to surrender Gimma and not the remainder of General Gazzera's forces. By not entering the town immediately it was hoped to force the surrender of all the remaining forces but this the Italians would not do and the Shifta forces of Ras Gurassu and Balambaras Zaude were dangerously close to its outskirts when 5th K.A.R. led Fowcol into Gimma early on 21st June.

Gimma yielded the usual haul of officers and men including General Sabatini, commander of the Italian Air Forces in Somaliland and General Daodiace (Vice Governor-General, Ethiopia) while General Bertello was taken a little later at Belletto, 20 miles out. Generals Gazzera and di Simone did not however surrender for some little time, and until further operations in which the 5th K.A.R. took no part, had been carried out against them.

On the 7th July Brigadier C. C. Fowkes issued the following Order of the Day which well sums up the operations in the Lakes area.

ORDER OF THE DAY

With the surrender of General Gazerra it must be expected that many of the units and sub-units which constituted Fowcol on its formation at Adama in May, or which have joined since, will disperse and rejoin their parent formations. And before they go I would like to express to everyone — of whatever rank or race — my warmest thanks and appreciation of their efforts which have contributed to the undoubted successes we have achieved.

In the course of a little less than two months we have marched 400 miles fought three major actions together with two limited actions and numerous advance guard and patrol engagements. As a result of these operations we have captured about 25,000 prisoners, 85 guns, 11 tanks and innumerable machine guns, rifles, etc. Our bag has included 12 generals, some complete with their staffs, and many other senior officers. It would probably be safe to estimate the casualties we have inflicted as nearly 1,000. At no time was Fowcol more than 6,000 strong and our own casualties were under 100.

Results such as these, even though the enemy we encountered was not of high quality, cannot be attained by the efforts or skill of any one arm or branch of the service. All have played their part; be it the staff who worked out the plans, assaulting infantry with the artillery and A.F.V.'s who supported them, the sappers, the supply columns and the medical units who cared for our wounded and sick. I would like all ranks to know, not only the measure of successes, but also that their individual grit and hard work fully contributed to our share in the final collapse of the enemy.

Signed,

C. C. FOWKES,

Brigadier.

Commander, 22nd East African Infantry Brigade.

For the 5th K.A.R. Gimma was the end of the operations in East Africa. Here they stayed for six months, sending off "D" Coy to Addis Abeba to assist in the evacuation of the Italians, and "A" Coy to Lines of Communication duties at Dalle. Shortly after the occupation the garrison was inspected by The Emperor of Abyssinia; his triumphal entry to the town was rather marred by the African sentries on the gate refusing to let him in until a British Staff Officer in his retinue hurriedly vouched for the Emperor's identity. It is understood that the visit was officially described as only a "qualified success".

At Gimma too the Battalion received the nucleus of its signal platoon under Lt. J. S. Adams. Until then the only signal equipment were some field telephones and No. 18 Wireless Sets. Whether due to comparatively untrained operators, or the general nature of the country, or the bumping about in the lorries these sets were never very reliable and operations were usually based on the assumption that they would'nt work. If they did it was a pleasant surprise.

Life in the garrison town was very pleasant, though at first there were many administrative duties in connection with the larger prisoner of war camps that had to be established, containing something like eight thousand men. Gradually as these prisoners were evacuated to Kenya and other places life settled down to routine guard duties and a little mild training chiefly against attack by paratroopers. Local ponies and horses were found and Polo and Paper Chasing instituted. In November an excellent gymkhana Race Meeting was organised which was attended by a number of visitors some from as far away as Addis Abeba. A weekly Newspaper "The Gimma Times" was started by Lt. R. A. Douglas-Pennant and had the distinction of being the first British Newspaper to be published in Ethiopia. Officers and men were all well housed and the stay in Gimma was very welcome after the exertions of the last year, but all good things come to an end and on Boxing Day the Battalion advance party consisting of "D" Coy with company representatives set off on the long trek back to Kenya via Maji and Lake Rudolph. This road had been surveyed by the Italians but never actually made up and consequently as the Battalion moved down it a few days later it soon started to break up, exceptional efforts being required to get some of the transport up the wet and slippery hills. There were two casualties on this march. Lt. Davies contracting Black water fever and later dying in Lokitaung Hospital, and Sgt. Ochola breaking his back when a vehicle overturned. The Battalion was glad to move by this route for it completed for them the Grand Tour of Abyssinia, in, as it were, by the front door and out by the back. Lt. Col. Hurt had most unfortunately to relinquish command of the Battalion owing to ill health at the end of December, Major Tweedie assuming command while the Battalion was at Todenyang on the shores of Lake Rudolph. There the Battalion remained for nearly three months, with one company on the Western shore of the Lake at Ileret, and other distributed along the Eastern edge doing garrison duty in the Merrille country, which had been disturbed by bands of Abyssinians armed with Italian weapons. They did not, however, have anything very much to do, except occasional patrols which was all to the good as the climate was unpleasantly hot.

Eventually the Battalion moved down country and found itself stationed at Yatta, Kenya, in March 1942 and the Abyssinian adventure was over for good and all.

CHAPTER 7.

THE CAMPAIGN IN MADAGASCAR

Arrived at Yatta the whole Battalion African and European were given leave and on their return re-equipment and training started in earnest. It was learnt that the Battalion would proceed overseas but of course the destination was unknown. This news was not well received by the African ranks, whose view was that Europeans fought in Europe, Africans in Africa and presumably Indians in India. The proximity of the Wakamba reserve too was a lure which proved too much for some of that tribe, however in the end their natural commonsense reasserted itself and it was in good heart that the Battalion embarked on June 3rd 1942 for their unknown destination, which of coursed proved to be Madagascar, under command of Lt. Col. P. A. Morcombe, who had taken over from Major Tweedie, on 31st March.

The sea voyage was the first that most of the African personnel had ever undertaken and their reactions were strange and numerous, some asserting that the patent log at the stern was the string by which the vessel could find its way back to Mombasa, others that it proceeded by means of stilts afixed to its bottom. Although the voyage was calm the African did not prove himself much of a sailor and for the first day or two conditions below decks were unpleasant. It was with the greatest difficulty that sufferers could be made to "take the air" on deck. However before long they all settled down and began to enjoy the novelty of the experience.

On arrival at Diego Suarez the Battalion took over from the the 2nd Btn. Northamptonshire Regt. and at the same time took over the Carriers which were an entirely new toy. The Battalion was lucky in having the best of the stations in that hot and unattractive area being posted to the old French Barracks at Orangea, near the headland that guards the narrow entrance to port. Here there was a magnificent beach within a stone's throw of Battalion Headquarters which was the scene of regular evening bathing parties. At the back and on the high ground were the old French fortifications built by General Joffre in his younger days and reminiscent of the style of 1870. Embedded in the cliff face of the narrows were three of the most enormous guns, which apparently had no traverse. but looked big enough to blow up a battleship even of modern build. Unfortunately we never saw them fired as they all had shells stuck half way up the barrels. Around and about were numerous lighter batteries each with its "Glacis" and served by a light railway running well below ground level. Altogether it was an extremely fine, for its period, piece of military engineering one could not help wondering against whom these formidable defences had been prepared. While at Diego "C" Coy carried out what is believed to be the first "Combined Operation" in K.A.R. History by making a seaborne assault landing on Mayotte the largest of the Comoro Islands. In this operation which captured the entire garrison (and a very excellent cook as well) Lt. Sheriff was awarded the Military Cross for conspicuous gallantry.

In August the Battalion moved South to Sakaramy for Brigade training prior to the second phase of the operations in Madagascar.

At that time it was not known whether the Brigade were to take part in these operations or sail to join the brigade already in Ceylon and speculation was rife. One officer of another unit so convinced that Ceylon was the destination in an earnest attempt at security gave it out that we were proceeding to Majunga (which of course we were) to capture the rest of the island. This was an unfortunate lapse but to restore the situation the Brigadier immediately withdrew all French coinage giving out that new coinage would be issued on board after we had sailed. This was a stroke of genius and after that there was no more talk of operations in the island.

Early in September the Brigade set sail, again for an unknown destination, and after taking a circuitous route was off Majunga on the morning of the 10th. The only incident of interest in this short sea voyage was the linking up at sea with another convoy from the mainland. As the two convoys approached each other a sort of mad circus, or so it seemed to the lay man, began with ships going round and round in circles. It was quite fascinating to watch the combined formation gradually taking shape and steaming off on their course.

The assault landing at Majunga was carried out by British Commandos and the 1st K.A.R. against a token resistance, 5 K.A.R. did not take part and disembarked some hours later in the normal manner.

Then followed a tiresome period of waiting for nearly three weeks while 1 K.A.R. raced up the road to the Capital Tananarive, carrying all before them. This period of waiting was due to the limited facilities for off loading the ships in the harbour but it must be admitted that there was something of the old "order and counter order" about the proceedings as on several occasions ships were brought along side for off loading and then promptly sent back to deep water and another brought in instead. It was commonly supposed that the Bills of Lading had got mixed up but this was probably untrue.

The 22nd Brigade, now under Command of Brigadier W. A. Dimoline (Brigadier Fowkes having been promoted to Major General Commanding 12 "A" Div.) was organised into three fighting groups each of one Battalion with a selection of supporting arms. The Battalion with its share of supporting arms formed the second fighting group but was last in order of battle and thus last to get the stores off loaded, so it was not till the 30th Sept. that they received orders calling them forward to take over from the 3rd group, the 6th K.A.R., at Antsirabe the fashionable "watering resort" some ninety miles South of the Capital.

Meanwhile the Battalion had not been completely out of the picture, for "D" Coy and some supporting arms under the second in Command, Major Tweedie, had been despatched North from Majunga to intercept a mythical Major Lanno who was said to be coming South with a party to cut the Majunga—Tannanarive Road, and to sandwitch him between themselves and the South Africans who were driving South, overland, from Diego Suarez. As it happened the French party had already surrendered so the expedition was fruitless but a change from routine. The move to Tannanarive, was uneventful except for having to negotiate the demolished bridge over the Betsiboka River. This had been a magnificent steel suspension bridge the cables of which had been severed lowering the carriage way into the river which, at that time of the year, was shalow. The engineers had rendered the bridge serviceable by piling sandbags on the portion below the water line but by the time the Battalion arrived the extra weight had caused the bridge to sag even more and it required considerable skill to drive the heavily laden vehicles up the steeply sloping carriageway.

Few drivers were capable of taking their lorries over this hazard, and a team of reliable men was organised to drive the convoy through; even so, some lorries ran backwards and the more heavily laden had to be assisted by towing and man handling.

After a brief halt at Tannanarive the group moved on to Antsirabe which was reached on the 2nd October. Here the Battalion stayed for a week carrying out various patrols and light duties while the 3rd group were pushing slowly forward clearing road blocks and generally mopping up. At last on the 9th the word "go" was given and off the group went to meet the first enemy positon a few miles South of

Ilaka. This was soon disposed of by a flank attack from a platoon of "C" Coy under Lt. Barkas together with a frontal attack by "D" Coy under Capt. Delap.

Meanwhile the signal officer Capt. Adams with the Intelligence Officer Capt. J. W. Howard had run into a nasty ambush while driving in a signals vehicle. Two askaris were killed and eight wounded; the two officers escaped unwounded although a burst of machine gun fire came through the cab of the vehicle between them.

From now on the road was heavily blocked every mile and sometimes every half mile, with stone and timber barricades anything up to eight feet wide and six feet high. Where it passed through a wood the trees had all been felled across it. Progress was therefore very slow the average day's advance being about five to ten miles with an occasional skirmish to add spice. Fortunately the enemy had not placed booby traps in any of these obstacles which would have made the business more tedious than ever but as it was it took from half to three quarters of an hour to clear a passage through the blocks sufficient for the transport.

The next objective of importance was the town of Ambositra, said to be the centre of the wine industry and one which of course the group was anxious to reach. Air reconnaissance had reported enemy positions at Antanjona just North of the town so "C" Coy were sent on foot around and behind the enemy positions to occupy Ambositra and cut off the enemy withdrawal. After a strenuous march through the hills to the West, spending one night on the heights in considerable discomfort they descended the precipitous hillside at dawn on the 13th and took the town completely by surprise before ever the battle to the North had started.

During the morning of the 12th, while the forward troops were pushing slowly down the road to Antanjona, "A" Coy in the lead with a section of Armoured Cars came on a concealed French 75 which let the first car pass and opened up on the second at 70 yards scoring a direct hit killing four askaris, and wounding ten others. Lt. Williamson of "A" Company was seriously wounded but subsequently recovered. Sgt. Seymour, also of "A" Coy, appreciating the position charged the gun position with the few men he could collect on the spur of the moment and knocked out the crew thus restoring the position. For this gallant act Sgt. Seymour was awarded an immediate Military Medal.

Proceeding forward next day patrols located enemy positions on both sides of the road one being slightly to the West of the road at Ambohipia and the other to the East in the area of the village of Antanjona as expected. After a sharp action in which Lt. Corbett Ward was killed, "D" Coy under Capt. Howard MC with a platoon of "B" Coy attached and cleared the position but the main defences on Antanjona proved too strong for "A" Coy alone and required a prepared plan. These positions were well sited, as indeed were all the French positions, on the forward slope of a ridge in front of which lay a rice paddy field, the strongest single feature being a tree clad salient covering, and directly to the East of, the main road.

For this prepared attack the Group was lent "D" Coy (Capt. Compton) of the 6th K.A.R. from the third group and a detachment from the 5th Commandos; it also had the support of the whole regiment of Field Artillery. The plan was a fairly simple left flanking movement, indeed this was about the only possible route, involving a long detour to gain the high ground to the East and at 17.15 hours the infantry attack went in led by Major Tweedie. After a short sharp engagement enemy bugles were heard sounding what seemed remarkably like "Cookhouse" and the enemy could be seen evacuating the positions not already overrun. By 18.30 hours the whole position was taken together with many prisoners, the Battalions casualties being three killed and eight wounded. Next day the column entered Ambositra. Here the Battalion spent some days clearing the road forward and patrolling a very strong enemy position held by some thousand troops overlooking the road at a point about six miles South. This position called for a Brigade attack and plans were laid accordingly. The 3rd Fighting group were sent around behind the main position to occupy Ivato while the 2nd group developed a surprise attack from the left flank on the heights of the Andriamanalina Ridge. Helped by an early morning mist the action went as planned and the enemy, taken completely by surprise and probably rather cold as well put up little fight. By midday the whole position had been cleared up and the troops were back in billets for lunch.

This swift and neatly executed manoeuvre resulted in the Capture of Col. Metras and nearly all his garrison. During the preparations for this attack Capt. J. S. Adams again attracted to himself the attentions of another French 65 mm gun whilst laying a line by signal truck. The driver sitting beside him was killed though he and the signal sergeant, Sgt. Wood, escaped injury and were eventually able to capture the gun in question. After this second effort lifts on signal vehicles were generally refused.

Before leaving Ambositra tribute must be paid to the welcome given the troops by the British and pro-British community, notably by Miss Hanning whose hospitality and kindness was very much appreciated by all ranks.

The 3rd fighting group were now in the lead and 5 K.A.R. followed on in reserve until Ambohimasoa where they again took over the advance, encountering some resistance from a French Company under command of a Capt. Malgorm the position being turned by "B" Coy. Most of the enemy escaped through the bush but later surrendered to "C" Coy who were pushing along the heights to the left of the road. At dusk that night, the 28th October, "C" Coy came up against resolute resistance by Capt. Gallibert and his company at the cross roads just beyond Ambatovaky. After a quick reconnaissance "C" Coy attacked in strength and overran the position killing fifteen of the enemy and capturing the rest. The advance continued through the night reaching Alakamisy at one o'clock in the morning where a French Colonel and a number of other prisoners were caught in bed. At first light "A" Coy continued the drive and thrusting aside the road blocks which were not so numerous as before entered Fianarantsoa, "the capital of the South" that afternoon. The entry into this town was a bit irregular in that the column was led in by the Second in Command and Intelligence Officer in a most disreputable old truck loaded with their personal servants and a number of squawking ducks and geese, much to the astonishment of the good citizens of Fianarantsoa. The Brigadier and Staff following closely behind the leading troops politely ignored the French Officials gathered at the outskirts for a ceremonial entry and drove on in without more ado. The French Engineer Officer responsible for road blocks and demolitions had left his departure too late and was caught by the Adjutant trying to make good his escape to the South.

Two days were spent at Fianarantsoa and then the Battalion left again for what was to prove the last lap of the journey down the Island. The road South from Fianarantsoa had been very heavily blocked and going was slow. At Antanandava the country opened out into something like moorland and for the first time the Carriers under Lt. Watson were able to go into action. After fighting a smart skirmish action the enemy were forced to withdraw leaving behind some very useful motor cars which were promptly annexed for Company Commanders use.

Later that afternoon while patrolling and mopping up the area was still going on, a sniper, using as was afterwards discovered a telescopic sight, killed Lt. Evans the Mortar Officer. This was really a very sad affair for it was just about the last shot of the campaign, the enemy surrendering without further fighting. But that is to anticipate.

The last enemy positions to be encountered before Ambalavao were at Vatoavo, and very strong indeed they were The road led down a valley closed at its Southern end by a horseshoe of bare hills, through which the road to Ambalavao passed by way of a col. The enemy were thoroughly dug into these hills their positions being connected together by underground passages. As the ground was open on all sides and provided a fine field of fire there did not seem very much chance of getting them out without tanks if they had a determined mind to stay there. However nothing daunted. "C" Company under Major Kemble decided to have a go, and, choosing the right flank, could be seen winding their way up the hillside, supported by artillery fire, while the remainder of the Battalion advanced rather gingerly down the main road. For some unexplained reason, perhaps to show they were still alive, the French opened up on an unoccupied village at the foot of the pass but stopped after a brisk fusilade of all arms. At half past three in the afternoon "C" Coy had reached their start line on the heights and were preparing for the very unpleasant task of an advance across the open and presumably bullet swept ground.

The Field Regiment opened heavy fire on the enemy but almost immediately bugle calls could be heard echoing around the hills. For some time the artillery concentrations continued until someone realised that the French were sounding the ceasefire. Our guns then closed and "C" Coy advancing at the double swarmed down over the hills to the French Headquarters where they were met by Capt. Meyer of the French Army who explained that he had just received news from his C.O. Major Bernasconi at Ambalavao, that General Guillemet the Officer Commanding the French Forces had ordered the "Cease Fire".

Unfortunately the telephone line back to Ambalavao had by now been cut, but Capt. Meyer stated that a Staff Officer was waiting there with an "important message" (the phrase is by now familiar) for the British Commander. Next morning acting on this message a small force from the fifth K.A.R. with two Staff Officers and News Reel Camera men walked ahead into Ambalavoa. Major Bernasconi, however, insisted in seeing the Brigadier in person who arrived an hour or two later when the road blocks had been cleared. An Armistice was arranged for 2 o'clock that afternoon the 4th November and a telephone call to Ihosy, Headquarters of the French Governor of Madagascar, M. Annet, brought his A.D.C. to Ambalavao by air; then followed a long period of negotiations and argument by the French representatives who seemed to be trying to spin out time for no apparent reasons. Finally at one minute past midnight, in other words on the 5th November, the Armistice was signed. It transpired later that under French law a campaign must be six months in duration to qualify for a "campaign medal" and the plenpotentiaries were under orders not to sign till the morning of the 5th November which would be exactly six months from the date of the original British landing in the North of the Island.

The Madagascar Campaign was now over and 5 K.A.R. though last to start had their fair share of the fighting and were in at the kill.

At Ambalavao the troops were most warmly welcomed, especially by the English Missionaries, Miss Buck and Miss Loughton, who placed their homes at the disposal of the officers and billeted many of the troops in their grounds.

Physically the campaign had been a good one with no undue hardship and plenty of fresh poultry to be had for the asking but it was not a pleasant undertaking as one could not help feeling that one ought not to be fighting erstwhile allies and that casualties on both sides were a needless waste of gallant lives.

CHAPTER 8.

INTERLUDE

Shortly after the Armistice the battalion moved back to Tananarive to take over garrison duties from 1/1 (Ny) K.A.R. The route followed was the same as that taken during the advance, escort duties being carried out as far as Antsirabe.

The battalion was in high spirits, conscious of a job well done, and looking forward to the amenities of the city. All enjoyed the peaceful move through such lovely country There had been little time or scope to appreciate its beauty during the hurried advance of the previous few weeks.

Tananarive proved to be a delightful station — a tonic to all. The French residents were friendly and hospitable though at first there was difficulty in finding out who were "Free French" by inclination and who by circumstance. Dances and sundowner parties were organized by Battalion Headquarters and by Companies, by way of return hospitality, and were well attended by the residents. In March 1943 The Deuxieme Battalion di Marche de L'Oubangi Shari — a Fighting French formation from Bir Hakim arrived in the capital and the Battalion was glad to be able to entertain them. These fighting Frenchmen were a most delightful set of people with many colourful stories of their adventures in North Africa. The 1/3 K.A.R. (Armed Car Regt.) also arrived at Tananarive about this time and it was a great pleasure to us to meet so many old friends a pleasure shared by British and African ranks alike. Much inter Battalion visiting and entertainment ensued.

The Askari undoubtedly enjoyed being at "Tan" as the city was nicknamed, and few will forget the sight of askari "walking out" in rickshaws pulled by the local native. They had won the campaign and intended that the Malagache should not forget it.

Although thoroughly enjoying itself the Battalion did not neglect its training and despite numerous garrison guard duties time was found to build a Battle Course, Carrier Course, and Battle Drill Camp, the last some twenty miles outside the town. The exercises provided by these courses were difficult perhaps even dangerous to the more elderly and less athletic. However none were seriously injured. It was by now fairly evident that the next active operations in which the Battalion was likely to take part would be against the Japanese in South East Asia and consequently all training was based on jungle warfare.

Sand table schemes, Tactical exercises without troops, and field exercises were held which were by no means unenjoyable. No member of the Brigade or Battalion had actual experience of jungle warfare, as opposed to Bush Warfare, and so interest was maintained. In addition to this training ceremonial parades were held on 19th December for inspection by the G.O.C. Islands Area, Maj. Gen. G. R. Smallwood and on the 5th January 1943 by the G.O.C. in C. East Africa Command Lt. Gen. Sir William Platt. The Battalion was also privileged to line the streets of Tananarive and provide the Guard of Honour for the state arrival of the High Commissioner, General Le Gentilhomme.

The Battalion handed over garrison duties to the 1/6 (TT) K.A.R. on the 3rd April and left for the Brigade jungle warfare camp at Vohipara. This camp was not pleasant nor indeed could it be since it was intended to represent jungle conditions, and a month's hard training followed. Although the Battalion was the last of the brigade to be exercised in this camp no short cuts were taken. Lessons were, in the main learnt by trial and error and in particular, attention was given to the experimental loading of men and vehicles. The knowledge gained was to stand us in good stead sooner than we expected.

Since the Armistice the Battalion had lost, from one cause or another, a number of British personnel amongst whom may be mentioned Major T.C.C. Lewin and Captain P. D. McEntee both on transfer and Captain N. W. Duirs, and Company Sergeant Major Caird on release. Thus the Battalion found itself short of British ranks during its jungle training and opportunity was taken to train African non-commissioned officers in practical map reading and platoon leading in the jungle. Amongst other exercises a 48 hour jungle compass march was carried out by these Africans with the most creditable results. It was also satisfactory to note how quickly the askari adapted themselves to the new conditions and although they did not like being in the jungle without the presence of British personnel, it brought out the power of leadership amongst the junior N.C.O.'s in a remarkable manner.

On the few days off training which the programme allowed visits were made to the neighbouring town of Ambositra where British ranks were most kindly welcomed by the European residents and football against the Malagache organised for the Africans.

The final "passing out" exercise under the direction of the Brigade Commander, Brigadier W. A. Dimoline, was held early in May with the co-operation of 56 Fd. Bty. R.A., and C Sqn. 1/3 K.A.R. Armd. Car Regiment. 1/(Ny) Bn.

K.A.R. acted as the enemy. The satisfactory conclusion of this exercise was celebrated in the time honoured way with large "ngomas".

After handing over the jungle camp to the care of the 1/1 (Ny) K.A.R. the Battalion was split up and so remained until early in the new year of 1944. Battalion Headquarters with Headquarter Company, C and D Companies moved to Fianarantsoa for garrison and escort duties, while A and B Companies under command of Major W. D. Draffan, were sent to garrison Tulear, the seaport on the South West of the Island. Early in June further dispersal took place with the departure to Mayotte Island of one platoon from D Company under Lieut. R. A. Douglas Pennant.

While at Fianarantsoa Mr. Fazan, C.B.E., representing the East African Governors' Conference, visited the Battalion to bring to the askari the latest news from their home districts. A brigade sports meeting was also organised at Fianarantsoa while further north at Antsirabe a most enjoyable race meeting was held which was attended by a number of officers and others from the battalion.

Late in July the Battalion, less the detachments at Tulear and Mayotte, sailed for Diego Suarez embarking at Tamatave on the S.S. Khedive Ishmael. The Battalion's motor transport proceeded by the overland route from Tananarive. At Diego Suarez the Battalion carried out normal training combined with garrison duties and guards. In December, however, this rather dull life was relieved by quite an exciting and difficult incident. The 1 Bn. The Mauritius Regiment also stationed in the area, got out of hand and burnt down their quarters. The 5 (K) K.A.R. from the South and the 1/1 (Ny) K.A.R. from the North were detailed to restore order. To ensure that no unfortunate incidents should occur from undue zeal on the part of the African askari, British ranks from the 3 (K) K.A.R. and 1/6 (TT) K.A.R. were drafted to the battalion taking part in the operation, and took over command of sections of askari. After a long and tiring, but not unamusing, day the main offenders were rounded up and taken to another camp under command of the 3 (K) K.A.R. The rest of the Mauritian Battalion remained in what was left of their own camp under guards provided by the 1/1 (Ny) K.A.R.

The usual festivities went on at Christmas time, including another Brigade Sports which the Battalion team won with some ease.

The period spent at Diego Suarez saw many changes take place in the composition of both the Brigade and the

Battalion. Our old friends the 1/6 (TT) K.A.R. were transferred to the 27 (EA) Inf. Brigade and were replaced by the 3 Bn. The Northern Rhodesian Regiment. Glad as we were to welcome this fine unit we could not but regret the loss of the 1/6 (TT) K.A.R. who, with the 1/1 (Ny) K.A.R., had trained and fought alongside us since the early days of the war. A fine team spirit had been built up between the three battalions, as well as many personal friendships, and it was hard at the time to understand the reasons for the change. In fact it was due entirely to territorial reinforcement difficulties. In addition to this loss we were also deprived of the services of our Brigadier, who was replaced by Brigadier Hendricks. In the Battalion itself, Captain J. W. Howard was recalled by the Kenya Government to take over the civil duties of District Commissioner, Mandera. Capt. Howard, a popular and efficient officer, had been on the staff of Battalion Headquarters since the beginning of the Abyssinian campaign, first as Intelligence Officer and later, after the Armistice at Ambalavoa, as Adjutant. His recall to civil duty was a loss to the Battalion and keenly felt by all his many friends. Capt. A. C. K. Barkas, son of Lt. Col. (now Brigadier) Barkas the Battalion's Commanding Officer at the outbreak of war, was appointed Adjutant. (His remark that he couldn't possibly be an Adjutant as he hadn't got a fountain pen availed him nothing.)

By the end of 1943 the Battalion's tasks in Madagascar were drawing to a close and it was with great delight that we learnt we were due to return to Kenya early in the New Year. Eventually the Battalion, less the Companies still at Tulear, embarked on the s.s. Ekma landing in Kenya in mid January 1944, and in due course found itself once more back at Yatta. Shortly after its arrival there, A and B Coys rejoined the Battalion having sailed direct from Tulear, and all ranks were sent on long leave during February and March.

The Garrison at Tulear had consisted of :—

    A and B Coys 5 (K) K.A.R. (Major W. D. Draffan)

    Detachment 5 (K) Field Ambulance.
    (Capt. J. Buchan, R.A.M.C.)

    16 (E.A.) Coast Defence Battery R.A. (Capt. J. Ankatell) and dependant on the situation either one or two squadrons R.A.F. with ground staff under F/O Ingles.

As only one infantry company was required for routine guards and duties, the other company was able to get on with training and much valuable work was done, not the least of which was the opportunity taken to teach all African ranks to swim.

The garrison was lucky enough to be able to acquire a Life Boat in which many pleasant afternoons were spent. This boat had come ashore, with survivors from a torpedoed American vessel, about one hundred miles North of Tulear. Major T. R. King, O.C. "B" Coy, went up with motor transport to bring in the survivors and Lt. Warton gallantly sailed the craft down the coast. At the end of June Major Draffan went on leave and Major King took over Command of the Garrison which he retained until the Companies rejoined the battalion in January 1944.

Tulear was a pleasant enough place and being something of an "outpost" it received a number of visits from distinguished people, including the General Officer Commanding Islands Area, Major General Smallwood, who was accompanied by the Brigade Commander, Brigadier W. A. Dimoline, Major General Size and Brigadier Taullec of the Fighting French Medical Services, and M. Le Contre — Admiral Anboynaeu, Commissaire National a la Marine. For all these and many others, guards of honour had to be provided. By and large life at Tulear was pleasant and easy, and it was with regret that Major King learnt that his request for a posting as permanent garrison Commander could not be approved. No account of Tulear however brief, would be complete without mention of Miss H. Foord, who organized and ran a troops canteen with great success. Miss Foord was a gay and charming personality who will long be remembered by all who served at Tulear.

By the beginning of April most of the Battalion had returned from leave and training and re-equipping started in earnest, continuing for the next two months. The G.O.C. in C. came down in June to inspect the Battalion in training and took the opportunity to present R.S.M. Ali Hersi with the Long Service and Good Conduct Medal. The end of June found the Battalion once more re-equipped and ready for the field and on 10th July, 1944 we sailed with the remainder of the Brigade for Ceylon.

The voyage on the whole was uneventful though it was with considerable pleasure we heard, when two days out from Mombasa, that Major General C. C. Fowkes, our old Brigade Commander and now Commanding the 11th (EA) Division, had asked for and been given the 5(K) K.A.R. as his Divisional Reconnaissance Battalion for the Divisions forthcoming operations against the Japanese in Burma. The only other excitement was the sight of one of the escort vessels leaving the convoy to drop depth charges. The vessel, however, soon returned to her station in the convoy which dropped anchor at Colombo on the 22nd. 5 (K) K.A.R. did not however disembark until the 24th.

The Battalion remained in Ceylon for about a fortnight, being stationed at Horana some 30 miles South of Colombo, but there was very little time to see much of the Island as the time was fully occupied in unpacking stores and sorting out those which would not be required for the Battalion's new role. In addition the whole Battalion had to be issued with a new type of lightweight bottle green battle dress which was in current use throughout the 14th Army Command.

The 5 (K) Battalion K.A.R. sailed for Calcutta on the 10th August 1944 aboard the s.s. Jalogopal, quite one of the dirtiest ships ever to sail the seven seas. The voyage only took seven days but that was quite long enough under such filthy conditions. Two days were spent in Calcutta at the Alipore Transit Camp before the Battalion entrained for the Bramaputra, where it embarked on the river steamer Ardfin on August 21st, subsequently transhipping to two crafts the Merlin and the Mersey, arriving at Pandu on the 23rd. This trip up the Bramaputra was most enjoyable and everyone was able to rest and relax after the rush and bustle of the previous few weeks. It is a trip that will be remembered by all ranks, especially the cool nights on deck, with the ship's searchlight picking up the navigating beacons as they steamed peacefully upstream.

At Pandu we struck heat and filth untold. The train was in such a disgusting state that the 2nd in Command refused to take it over until it had been properly cleaned, which took four hours. However the Battalion eventually left for Dimapur not thinking very much of India so far. At Dimapur it embussed immediately for Palel which was reached safely after a hair raising drive. There rear Divisional Headquarters were contacted and we came under direct command of 11 (EA) Division for the first time since the Abyssinian days.

CHAPTER 9.

BURMA — WEST OF THE CHINDWIN RIVER.

Part I THE APPROACH MARCH — PALEL TO CHINYAUNG 1 Sep. — 14 Oct. 1944.

Part II THE ACTION AT LETSEGAN 22 OCT. 1944.

Part III NYAUNGBIN TO THE CHINDWIN — NOV. 1944.

Part IV OPERATIONS OF DRAFFORCE — NOV. 1944.

Part V OPERATIONS OF "C" COMPANY — NOV. 1944.

PART I

The Approach March — Palel to Chinyaung
1 Sep. — 14 Oct. 1944.

At Palel it was learnt that the advanced elements of the Division were in the general area of Sunle seventy-five miles to the South. It was necessary to get forward on foot as fast as possible, making a first bound of about forty miles to a point known as Bulldozer Ridge where main Divisional Headquarters were established.

Since the Battalion, only took with it Jeeps and trailers, reorganisation was again necessary and here the training in the jungle camp in Madagascar proved its value. Kit and stores which could not be taken were dumped in tents and left in charge of a small rear party. It was generally thought that after this reorganisation the Battalion was down to an irreducable minimum of kit, although in fact, before the operations were over, it was to lose contact with the Jeeps and be on an even lighter scale of equipment, without any apparent loss of efficiency. Before leaving, sections from each Company under an officer (A. McDonald, B. Armitage, C. Woolcombe, D. Thomson, and H. Q. Senior) were sent forward for attachment to the units of the 25th (EA) Inf. Brigade for the purpose of gaining experience in patrol work. These sections did indeed carry out valuable patrols but were so overworked that the majority of the men had to be evacuated to hospital with fever or foot-rot as soon as they rejoined their companies; this was unfortunate as they had no time to pass on to their cmorades the valuable lessons learnt.

The march to Bulldozer Ridge took three days. The track ran across the grain of the country and heavy rain fell most of the time. The last fifteen miles onto the ridge were mainly uphill and arduous in the extreme. Under these conditions the practice of marching for fifty minutes and resting for ten was impracticable and the routine was according to the state of the track and the gradient, sometimes with only twenty minute intervals between rests. This march did much to harden up the Battalion after the long journey from Kenya and it says much for the general fitness of all ranks that casualties were very few.

At Bulldozer Ridge a few days respite were allowed from marching and the time used for field firing practice, there being a plentiful supply of ammunition left there by formations which had gone ahead.

The Monsoon was now at its height and marching conditions became worse and worse. The Battalion struggled down the Kabaw Valley through the mud and rain to within six miles of Sunle. Here the Sunle Chaung rose and swept away the bridges both behind and in front of the Battalion, cutting road communications completely. The food situation was grave but fortunately the 3/6(TT) K.A.R. were in the same area and were able to help out; in addition a number of water buffalo were shot for meat. These animals had been seen in a glade and were at first thought to be wild, it subsequently transpired that they were tame working beasts the property of the local natives. It became even more unfortunate when it was found that owing to a misunderstanding of orders a total of twenty two were shot instead of six. This affair not only incurred "The Divisional Commander's grave displeasure" but nearly provoked an international incident as the owners promptly took away their elephants which had been helping the engineers to repair the bridges. The difficulty was eventually overcome by paying excessive compensation. It was as well for all concerned that communications were down and the Divisional Commander prevented from making a personal appearance.

Meanwhile the Battalion's Advance Party (Maj. Draffan, Capt. Valentine, Warton and Charman, Lt. Mathews, Sgt. Paynter and sixteen African ranks) were in grave difficulties as they became totally marooned between Sunle and Hintzin. Although they were well off for food, having salvaged the Divisional Canteen before it was washed away with two other vehicles, they had an anxious time watching the water rise; indeed the situation became such that trees were selected up which to climb and store kit, but eventually they were not forced to this extremity.

When the floods abated the Battalion were given the task of remaking the road and gradually worked its way forward to Khampat fifteen miles south of Sunle. The work entailed the felling of trees to make a "corduroy" surface to the track along which wheeled traffic could just move. Altogether many miles of such roads were constructed by all Units thus enabling the Division to advance slowly down the valley. Although it was proposed to supply the Division by air, dropping supplies in bulk where needed, some sort of road was necessary to distribute these supplies and to permit the movement of ambulances, artillery and other essential vehicles.

While in the Sunle—Khampat area the Commanding Officer Lt. Col. P. A. Morcombe, O.B.E., went down with

Tick Typhus and had to be evacuated to hospital, the first stage necessitating a six mile hand carry by stretcher. The Colonel being seriously ill was evacuated to a base hospital in India and was never again able to catch up with the Battalion. This was a most unfortunate and unhappy way in which to leave the Battalion he had commanded for so long and with such success. Major W. D. Draffan took over command until the arrival of Major T. C. C. Lewin at Kintzin on October 1st. Major Lewin had, since leaving the Battalion in Madagascar, commanded the II (EA) Divisional Scouts and had seen action with them against the Japanese in the Arakan a few months previously.

During the flood period supplies had been brought forward by amphibious vehicles known as DUCKS. On one occasion a member of an off loading party, Pte. Thatheri was swept away by the flooded Khampat River. C.Q.M.S. Evans immediately dived in after him and despite the struggles of the drowning man brought him safely to the bank. It is a matter for regret that this gallant action did not receive official recognition.

At Khampat the Battalion was given its first operational directive by the Divisional Commander. The task was to clear the enemy from a dug in position on spot height 3069, a mile and a half East of the Lake and Rest House at Letsegan, which was threatening the left flank of the Division's Lines of Communication. To assist in the operation 101 Mortar Battery of 304 Field Regiment R.A. joined the Battalion at Chinyaung and "D" Company 44 (U) K.A.R. already at Letsegan came under Command. For transport mules were allotted and it was understood that at Letsegan two Elephants would also be detailed to assist. The general plan was to form a rear base at Chinyaung as from there on it would not be possible to take the Jeeps. The Battalion had never before operated with mule transport, nor could anyone remember receiving any instructions in their care and attention so their arrival presented a certain amount of anxiety particularly as the muleteers were all Indians which caused a language problem. As soon as the mules arrived and had been loaded according to a hastily prepared programme the Battalion set off down the road to Chinyaung. The going was very bad and the Jeeps although fitted with anti-skid chains on all four wheels frequently had to be man-handled for yards and even the mules required a certain amount of manual assistance from time to time. During the move the Jeeps succeeded in cutting the telephone line back to Divisional Headquarters. This in itself could easily have been put right had it been spotted in time but unfortunately night was coming on and the drivers seeing broken ends of wire lying about cut off great lengths to fix up their night bivouacs. For the second time the Battlion incurred the grave displeasure of the General. Our record to date had not been very bright but fortunately affairs at Letsegan were to turn out satisfactorily and such peccadillos forgotten.

Another incident less serious but distressing all the same occurred on the morning of the last day's march. As the column was forming up an Askari, who had been behaving peculiarly during the night, went clean off his head and removed all his clothing. In this naked condition but grasping his rifle he insisted in marching into battle with the column. All attempts to persuade him differently failed and it was only with the administration of drugs that he could be put onto a Jeep and sent under escort to the nearest Field Ambulance. At Chinyaung preparation and organisation commenced in earnest for the assault on Pt. 3069. The wheeled transport and stores not required for the action were placed under the Quartermaster Capt. A. Harper, as Officer Commanding Administration Company, and "C" Company were detailed to remain at Chinyaung as guard company. During this preparatory period enemy patrols were active in the area and "D" Company carried out the dual role of road maintenance and escort Company between Chinyaung and the Headquarters of the 26th (EA) Inf. Brigade on the main Yedok—Yazagyo road. It was on this track that Lt. Bunn, the Battalion Transport Officer had a narrow escape from ambush. He had set off early one morning to visit Brigade Headquarters and return immediately. Fortunately for him he was delayed at Brigade Headquarters, for in the interval the enemy laid an ambush on the track but were in turn discovered and driven off by a patrol from 2/2 (Ny) K.A.R. Lt. Bunn returned blithely to Headquarters shortly after this brisk action quite unaware of the events which had taken place.

On 16 October 1944 the Officer Commanding 101 Mortar Bty Major A. A. Makay, reported to Battalion Headquarters and his Unit arrived some hours later having been delayed by the state of the roads. The following morning the move to Letsegen commenced.

PART II

The Action at Letsegan — 22 Oct. 1944.

Chinyaung lies on the Western edge of the range of hills which divide the Kabaw and Chindwin valleys. The track to Letsegan runs across these hills rising some fifteen hundred feet in the seven miles between the two points. It was narrow and slippery from recent rain and had to be made passable to the mules by the Fieldworks Platoon under Lt. Mathews; the remainder of the Battalion giving assistance as required. Lt. Senior and his section, who had been attached to the 4/4 (U) K.A.R. since Palel, met the marching troops a mile out from Letsegan and guided them into the Headquarters of "D" Company of the 4/4 (U) K.A.R.

The enemy position on Pt. 3069 had been investigated by both this company and by the 2/2 (Ny) K.A.R. so that much useful information was already available though insufficient upon which to form a plan. Intensive patrolling therefore started immediately guides being initially supplied by "D" Company 4/4 (U) K.A.R. Lts. Stille and Seed both succeeded in reaching the enemy wire and observing his defences from close quarters. The country was however so broken and the cover so thick that it was difficult to pinpoint the position on the map or be certain of it from any distance away. The position was finally determined by a piece of good fortune. It had been arange that the Mortar Battery should range on the position at a time when all patrols would be clear. Their bombs however fell close to a patrol which was resting some three hundred yards away from the enemy defences and it was clear that they were on the wrong target. As a result of the information brought in by the patrol the next shoot fell accurately on the defences and we were at last able to tie them up with the map. (This early experience showed us the use of smoke bombs for registering concealed enemy positions. Unfortunately it did not always work out in practice as the Japs soon got wise to what we were doing and would put up their own smoke bombs on some other feature.)

On October 20th air support was requested for the first time and at 1400 hours that afternoon the enemy's position was heavily attacked by six Hurribombers. As far as could be seen the air strike was accurate but the density of the jungle prevented detailed observation of the result. Although the heavy Monsoon rains seemed to be easing up the weather was still difficult with occasional rain and much low cloud. It was never possible to foretell whether an airstrike would take place as ordered since aircraft might be fog bound on their landing ground or the target area might be obscured. As a target area had to be clear of all troops well before an airstrike, failure of the aircraft to arrive could constitute a waste of valuable time. The Battalion was lucky however and had few "misses".

By the evening of the 20th October sufficient information had been gained by patrols to complete a picture of the enemy's position and prepare a plan for an assault on the 22nd.

The enemy appeared to be established on two hills about two hundred yards apart, and astride the track from Letsegan to Mawlaik on the Chindwin River. Pt. 3069 was determined as being the most Easterly of the two features. The position was surrounded with barbed wire and defended by some fifty to sixty men in trenches and bunkers. Any approach from the North was quite out of the question as on this side the defended features were on the edge of a steep cliff which dropped almost sheer to the valley fifteen hundred feet below. On the other three sides it was possible to approach close to the wire which was only a single stranded upright fence and no great obstacle in itself. The trouble was however, that the sides of the hills were so steep, that, except where the track to Mawlaik crossed the saddle between them, it seemed impossible for troops to assault with any vigour. As it happened no single patrol had been completely round both hills in a continuous reconnaisance and it was naturally assumed that the features were mutually supporting and enclosed in a continuous belt of wire. In fact this was not the case.

The force based at the Rest House consisted of:

5 (K) K.A.R. less C. Coy.
D Coy. 4/4 (U) K.A.R. (Major I. Yorke-Davies).
101 Mortar Bty. 304 Fd. Regt. R.A. (Major Makay).
Detachment No. 2 (Z) Fd Ambulance. (Capt. Hall RAMC).

The general plan of attack provided for an Air Strike on the Western end of the enemy position folowed by a bombardment from the Mortar Battery. On completion of the bombardment "B" Company (Major Townley) were to launch a holding attack on the Western defences, which it was hoped would draw off some of the garrison from the Eastern end where the main assault would be made by "A" Company (Major Barkas) and "D" Company (Major

Howard MC) under the co-ordination of the Battalion second in command, Major Draffan, MBE. "D" Company 4/4 (U) K.A.R. were placed in reserve under Battalion Headquarters and given the initial role of blocking the track to Mawlaik so as to prevent evacuation or alternatively reinforcement by this route, forming a firm base for "A" and "D" Companies assault and providing local protection for Battalion Headquarters and the Regimental Aid Post. This plan involved an encircling movement by "A" and "D" Companies, known as ADFORCE for the purpose of the operation, "A" Company being on the right or outer flank of the wheel. Such was the nature of the terrain that it was thought unwise to attempt this movement by night; alternatively had the troops moved the previous day and lain up by night close to their start lines it was almost certain that they would have been discovered by Japanese patrols and the hoped for factor of tactical surprise lost. The operation was therefore timed to start with an air strike at 08.30 hours on the morning of the 22nd October.

The 21st was spent in reconnaisance by Company and Platoon Commanders of the exact route they would follow the next day, and in dumping forward of ammunition at the Mortar Battery's gun positions. As a result of these final patrols it was found that the route for "A" Company would have to be changed considerably which well illustrates the difficulty of planning an operation in that type of country broken as it was by a multiplicity of minor ridges and water courses known by the local name of "Chaung".

By now the Japanese were suspicious of our intentions and during the night of the 21/22 October the Fieldworks Platoon guarding the forward ammunition dump were harassed by enemy "jitter" parties and stood to all night. At dawn Lt. Mathews found three of his men missing. It transpired that they had not approved of the attentions of the Japanese and removed themselves to a quieter area. Their punishment was made to fit their crime and for the next ten nights they slept by themselves outside the perimeter of our defended localities. No further cases of scrimshanking troubled the Battalion.

Rain fell during the night and it was damp and miserable as the troops moved off to their start lines at dawn. Almost immediately there came a hitch in the plan : a small chaung had risen during the night and with the passage of troops the steep banks became increasingly slippery causing much delay. A quick decision was made to postpone all timings for the attack by one hour, though this meant we would lose the shock effect of the air strike which could not be postponed at such short notice. As it turned out even an hour's delay was insufficient. By 8 o'clock the weather had cleared and the air strike came in punctually at 8.30. Divisional Headquarters had done us exceptionally well and allotted us twelve Hurribombers though we had only called for six. Directed by a round of smoke from the Mortars the full weight of their attack fell as planned on the enemy's Western defences. Such was the accuracy and force of their bombing and machine-gunning that they laid bare a swathe of jungle around the enemy. In actual fact as the ground troops were not in a position to follow up the air attack while the enemy were still dazed and the resulting "Glacis" aided the Japanese more than ourselves. The next development was a harassed message from the Battery to say they were being attacked by a Japanese patrol of unknown strength. This was the Battery's first experience of active operations and caused them to take an unduly pessimistic view of their predicament. Nevertheless they soon recovered themselves and dealt with the intruders who withdrew in the face of the determined counter patrol sent out by the battery.

At 9.30 "B" Company crossed their start line and moved on their objective. "D" Company was also moving on time but no news could be obtained of "A" Company who were out of wireless touch owing to the thickness of the jungle interfering with reception. As soon as "B" Company made contact with the enemy, the battery brought down heavy and accurate concentration as planned. Here a most unfortunate accident happened. One bomb of the concentration fell far short wounding Major Townley, Lt. Cheyne and three askari (all of whom happily recovered later). To add to this setback and general confusion a stretcher bearer Sergeant from 2 (Z) Fd. Ambulance was shot whilst carrying Major Townley back for medical attention. This incident temporarily disrupted communications with "B" Coy as their wireless set was with Major Townley, however the Medical Officer was able to keep Battalion Headquarters in touch with events on "B" Company's front through his own set. Order was soon restored and the advance continued. On reaching the enemy defences the Company was held down by heavy fire and in spite of determined attempts were unable to work their way across the open ground. Mention must here be made of a Samburu Askari whose dead body was subsequently found within a few feet of an enemy machine gun post, he had obviously all but made his own private objective.

While this engagement was going on in the West, Adforce Headquarters reported that "D" Company was steadily closing on the enemy's eastern defences and were as yet undetected, but neither they nor "D" Company had any news of "A" Company. Just as Battalion Headquarters were wondering what on earth had happened to "A" Company firing was heard in their direction and shortly afterwards Adforce reported that "A" Company were in action. A few minutes later "D" Company were also engaged and the main battle was joined.

A fierce fight now developed in the thick jungle the enemy blasting away with all his automatic weapons and hurling bunches of grenades from his trenches and from men posted in the tops of trees. The visibility in the jungle was not more than twenty to thirty yards, but all wireless communications were working well, and the ground telephone lines still intact, so despite the lack of visibility Company Commanders were able to keep Battalion Headquarters well informed of what was happening on their fronts and Headquarters in turn were able to pass on the news to the other Companies and Units. This happy state of affairs did much to support morale and maintain the pressure of the attack, which might otherwise have faded out under the prevailing conditions.

During this period the Japanese persistent as always sent out snipers to take pot shots at Battalion Headquarters, but "D" Company 4/4 (U) K.A.R. soon detected them, killing one and wounding the other who however managed to get away.

By midday the critical phase of the attack was reached. On the Western side "B" Company were firmly held and suffering casualties, but performing the useful task of containing the enemy. On the eastern side "A" Company having suffered an estimated 50 per cent casualty rate could not make the last fifty yards, while "D" Company's two leading platoons, also having suffered casualties, were similarly held up on the edge of the enemy's perimeter.

on a bold move, withdrawing into reserve his mauled right flank platoon he launched his fresh and last platoon round his left flank straight up the gentle gradient of the Letsegan —Mawlaik track, between the two enemy held positions. Immediate success followed this movement and the platoon gallantly lead by African Platoon Commander Kipchoge swept over the wire and into the enemy lines. Sergeant

Bull commanding "D" Company's other leading platoon, taking advantage of the diversion caused by A.P.C. Kipchoges platoon scrambled up the steep slope facing him, forced the wire, and at the head of his men charged the enemy trenches. The Japs seeing their position over-run leapt screaming from their trenches and bunkers to charge like maniacs down the hill into "A" Company who killed the majority, twenty one dead bodies being subsequently counted in the area.

Point 3069 was thus in our hands by 1 o'clock but the the position facing "B" Company still held out. Major Draffan commanding Adforce immediately sent out one Platoon from "D" Company 4/4 (U) K.A.R., which had been sent up to him as his force reserve, to contain the enemy, while he set about consolidating the gains on Pt. 3069 and sorting out the Companies which had become pretty well mixed up. On learning of the fall of Pt. 3069 "B" Company were ordered to move round the Southern flank and come into reserve while the battery were at the same time directed to stand by for a final bombardment of the enemy prior to an assault.

Before this move could be completed the Japs, realising they were about to be destroyed, evacuated their position by the only possible route, over the edge of the cliff on the North. We found the marks they had left where they slid down on their behinds but how many reached the bottom safely we never knew. Suffice it to say that a patrol from 2/2 (Ny) K.A.R. who had previously been forced to take this way out when surprised by the enemy, suffered five casualties in the process.

This action at Letsegan has been described in considerable detail as it was the Battalion's first and most important action in Burma. The Adjutant's Battle Log is attached as an appendix.

Our casualties were :—

Officers killed	Nil
Officers wounded (Major Townley, Lts. Cheyne, McDonald, Seed)	4
B.O.Rs. Killed and wounded ...	Nil
Africans Killed	12
Africans died of wounds	2
Africans wounded	79

of the enemy 28 bodies were found in all but it is impossible to say how many other casualties they received. Amongst the African dead was C.S.M. Raguti of "A" Company a faithful Jaluo soldier of many years service. He was killed at the side of his Company Commander, Major Barkas, who himself had a narrow escape as his orderly was wounded at his other side, both casualties occuring within a few seconds of each other.

Readers of these notes who were not in Burma at this time may wonder why it was necessary to deploy a full Battalion against a position held by sixty men. This heavy concentration of troops on the ground did indeed increase the number of casualties caused by grenades. At the time of this action our troops had not as yet met such tough fighters as the Japanese and it was vitally necessary that their first action should be successful. The Commanding Officer, fresh from his experiences with African Troops in the Arakan, had in mind the deplorable consequences involved when their morale was lowered by early reverses and other causes.

The principle adopted therefore was to use as many troops as possible so that none should feel lonely and in addition to control the whole action with dual communications. Every unit taking part was linked by wireless and telephone line was also run out to the Battery, "B" Company and Adforce Headquarters. All Units were thus in close touch with Headquarters and they themselves by, a rear link, with Divisional Headquarters. The signal arrangements reflected the greatest credit on the Signal Officer, Lt. G. M. Allen, and his Section who laid over six miles of line through thick jungle in an hour, and who kept the system working at high efficiency. The success of the operation may be largely attributed to the ease with which orders and news could be distributed to those taking part. This in turn heartened all ranks so that they gave of their best, fully living up to their already high reputation for dash and gallantry. The initiative of the African non commissioned officers and men in this soldier's battle was of a high order, the Somali, Samburu, Nandi and Kipsigi, as might be expected, being particularly meritorious.

At least one story, typical of the African, relates how in this action a Nandi soldier with a "panga" in his right hand slew a Japanese and with his left hand searched him for a watch.

When the battle was over, "A" and "B" Companies which had suffered the highest casualties were left at Pt. 3069 as a garrison, their total strength being little more than one full Company, The remainder of the force made ready to return to Chinyaung. The evacuation of the wounded presented quite a problem as many were stretcher cases requiring at least four bearers each. The wounded were sent off in two batches, the most serious cases leaving on the 23rd being carried and escorted by personnel of the Mortar Battery. Owing to the walking wounded being unable to keep up on the rough going, the column did not reach Chinyaung until the 24th. The remainder of the wounded with the rest of the force arrived on the evening of that day also. This problem of evacuating wounded over jungle paths was always one with which to reckon in any operation. Four fit men, and eight if the carry was a long one, were required to carry one wounded man. Thus after a stiff action there might easily be insufficient fit men available to both consolidate the gains and evacuate the wounded.

At Chinyaung excellent arrangement for the reception of wounded had been made by 61 (Z) Field Ambulance (Capt. Kerton R.A.M.C.) in conjunction with "B" Company 13 (Ny) K.A.R. (Major Bell). Temporary huts had been rushed up and doctors with Jeep Ambulances driven by American volunteers were standing by.

On the day after the return of the main body to Chinyaung the Divisional Commander, with his G.S.O. 1 Lt. Col. Biggs, paid a complimentary visit to the Battalion. The sentry posted on the side of the track to direct the Divisional Commander to Battalion Headquarters was much too awed to stop a car bearing the Divisional Commander's flag with the result that the General overshot the turning. His greeting on arrival was typical of the "Kali" old man, "What the Devil do you mean by not having a guide to direct me? However you've had a good battle so I'll forgive you but don't do it again." All ranks were most gratified by the General's visit none more so than the Askari with whom he walked and talked. The General was evidently pleased with our performance and after having promised to send us our small requirements returned to his Headquarters. That evening a Jeep full of worried looking Staff Officers arrived. They said they had been sent for personally by the General who was of the opinion that from what he had seen the 5th K.A.R. were being shamelessly neglected, and if matters were not put right at once he'd sack the lot of them. They were calmed down and assured that the General was overestimating our needs, but it was nice to know that from then on the Battalion's requirements would have high priority.

As a result of the action at Letsegan the Commanding Officer and Sgt. Bull of "D" Company received immediate decorations, the former being awarded the Military Cross, the latter the Military Medal.

PART III

Nyaungbin to The Chindwin.

The occupation of Pt. 3069 removed the threat of an attack on the Division's left flank via the Mawlaik-Letsegan track, but similar tracks from the Chindwin existed further to the South and the Battalion less the garrison left at Letsegan were ordered to occupy Nyaungbin and prevent any enemy advance westwards via the Palusawa-Nyaungbin track.

"C" Company (Major Shaw) left for Nyaungbin a day ahead of the main body and although they found traces of a Japanese position estimated to have held twenty to thirty men, they encountered no opposition.

The track like that to Letsegan was narrow and had to be cleared for the mule transport. At one point it was lost altogether and the force arrived on the Bon Chaung a mile or more west of its destination. This involved a delay of nearly five hours and much difficult marching and cutting of tracks. Lt. Clough and his platoon had to cut a special path for the mules as they could not follow the route taken by the marching troops.

The position at Nyaungbin was on the top of a hill and pleasant enough. The rains were nearly over and the nights growing cold so the troops missed their jerseys which were back with the Quartermaster. However, tightly wrapped in gas capes they did not fare too badly. Below the position lay the remains of the Rest House at Nyaungbin and in a bend of the Bon Chaung an area was cleared as a dropping zone for air supplies.

The main danger to the position was a tall hill a mile to the South West which completely overlooked it and the dropping zone. To prevent the enemy occupying this hill unknown a section was posted on it as a picket. All went well until one afternoon an explosion was heard from the direction of the hill to be followed shortly by the arrival of two very frightened Africans who said the Japs had occupied the hill and driven them off. A strong patrol was immediately sent out to restore the position but returned with a very different story. It appeared that one of the picket while on sentry duty had inadvertently released a grenade thereby blowing himself up. The remainder of the picket hearing the explosion and seeing the sentry killed assumed the Japanese were upon them and took to their heels. In their hurry two of them fell over the edge of a cliff and were killed. From this incident were learnt the futility of posting small bodies of Africans without British ranks in isolated position no matter how strong.

As the main task was to hold the track at Nyaungbin the troops set about digging themselves in with a will, and generally strengthening a naturally good position. The Signal Officer, determined to have peace and quiet at any price, produced a remarkable fortification for himself and his signal centre, which was generally referred to as the "Kikuyu pigstye". By the time the defence works were completed the Force was under ground and proud of their first effort at "dug-outs". The "Dug-outs" were furnished with bunks and shelves made from split bamboo and teak slabs from the Rest House provided table tops. Taking a lesson from the Japanese at Letsegan the defences were surrounded with booby traps and "panjis" (sharpened bamboo stakes). The troops were full of confidence and it was cheering to hear them say "let 'em all come."

While these defensive works were being carried out patrols were sent far and wide. Sgt. Bull in attempting to get through to Paluzawa on the Chindwin ran into an enemy post at Wabobin about six miles up the track. This eventually turned out to be well sited and very strong position holding at first some forty men, later being strengthened to sixty. Another patrol under A.P.C. Kipchoge saw enemy near Chaungzon village but although they spotted the footprints of our patrol no action followed. While probing the depth and extent of the Wabobin position an African askari was killed. The following day a patrol attempted to recover the body which the Japs had pulled onto the track and stripped of its equipment. This was a deliberate trap as they had the body covered with light automatic weapons and opened up on the patrol as soon as they reached the body. Fortunately they inflicted no casualties.

The Wabobin position proved too strong for us to deal with, particularly as by now "C" Company had been sent off on detachment down the Bon Chaung. As a precaution against a surprise movement by the enemy "D" Company moved up on to a strong position astride the track just short of the enemy. Their task was to keep the enemy under close observation, harass them as much as possible, and deny them the approach to Nyaungbin, which was by now only lightly held by Headquarter Company and used for obtaining supplies by air. This task they manfully fulfilled and on the night of the 16th November the Japs pulled out. A final drop of supplies was taken at Nyaungbin and Bn. H.Q. and H.Q. Company closed up on "D" Company preparatory to moving to Chaunzon and thence to Palusawa. These moves were in accordance with the orders of the 21 (EA) Inf Brigade (Brigadier J. MacNab, D.S.O., O.B.E.) under whose command the Battalion less "C" Company had recently been placed.

While at Nyaungbin two Burmese bombardiers from the Burmese Intelligence Corps were posted to the Battalion. These two grand young men, called Twing and Claude, were most useful going on numerous patrols and organising the local Burmese for us. When war broke out they had been students studying engineering at Rangoon University. On the invasion of Burma they joined the Artillery and marched out with General Alexander's forces. After the evacuation, they with others of their type, were formed into the Burmese Intelligence Corps to assist in the re-occupation. All ranks became most attached to these two delightful characters who remained with the Battalion until the end of operations on the Chindwin. Loyal, courageous and cheerful they gave us of their best.

At Chaungzon a strange party of Africans under a British Officer and a Sergeant joined Bn. H.Q. They were a detachment from the Divisional Deception Unit, not heard of previously, and were full of enterpirse and conjuring tricks. By means of fire crackers and other devices they proposed to deceive the Japanese as to our real strength. Unfortunately it was not possible at this time to produce any Japanese for them to deceive so they were sent off with a suitable escort to look for some. After having staged a magnificent and completely bogus battle in the Palusawa Chaung they returned well pleased. Eventually they were wished off on to Headquarters 21 (EA) Inf Brigade who did not know what to do with them any more than Bn. H.Q., did. After carrying out a number of abortive patrols in the Chaungzon area, one of which reached Baingbin seven miles south, Bn. H.Q., "D" and H.Q. Coys closed on Palusawa where Brigade Headquarters were established.

The next task given was that of crossing the Chindwin and providing left flank protection for the advance of the brigade down the West bank. On the 20th November the river was crossed and at 18.00 hours that day the advance party, under the Commanding Officer, made contact with the second-in-command, Major Draffan, in the Masein area. This officer who had with him Major Culver as his Staff Officer, a small party of Battalion Signals under Sgt.

Pemble, and last but not least the invaluable Twing had left the Battalion at Nyaungbin to take command of the Letsegan Garrison. They had subsequently been ordered to leave Letsegan, cross the Chindwin at Mawlaik and act as flank protection for the leading elements of the brigade. This small force had been styled "Drafforce" and an account of its operations follows in Part IV of this chapter.

The Chindwin River at Paluzawa is about half a mile wide and the crossing was carried out on rafts and small boats, some of which were fitted with outboard engines and used to tow the remainder of the flotilla. The crossing was uneventful save for the difficulties experienced in ferrying the mules across. These were overcome by the Adjutant, Capt. H. H. Williamson, who put in some remarkably good work.

PART IV

Operations of Drafforce — November 1944.

The Garrison left at Letsegan, under the command of Major A. C. K. Barkas, consisted of "A" and "B" Companies 5 (K) K.A.R. "B" Troop, 101 Bty 304 Regiment R.A. (Mortars) (Capt. J. W. Thomas) One Detachment from No. 2 (Z) Field Ambulance (Capt. J. E. Kerton) and a detachment of 11 (EA) Divisional Signals. When the Battalion moved south to Nyaungbin the garrison was placed under 13 (Ny) K.A.R., whose headquarters were at Chinyaung. Their task was to hold Point 3069 at all costs and to patrol the area so as to give early warning of any Japanese advance.

The garrison occupied the old Japanese position, one company being on each feature, but soon developed it out of all recognition. Extensive wiring was carried out and the trench system increased so that all parts of the position could be reached without a head being shown above ground. Everyone slept below ground in a veritable rabbit warren.

The approaches and any unoccupied part of the area were heavily booby trapped. The 3 inch Mortars, sited in each of the two main areas were given short range tasks, and by firing with their primary charges could land their bombs within fifty yards of the defences. The clearing made by previous air attacks was extended and turned into a dropping zone for air supply, and, although this was very close to the cliff edge on the North, only once were any supplies lost. In addition to numerous routine patrols, such as keeping open the Letsegan—Chinyaung track (carried out alternatively from either end) and watching other likely approaches, many long distance patrols were sent out to keep contact with the flank of the enemy who were putting up a stubborn resistance to the advance of the 21 (EA) Inf Brigade along the west bank of the Chindwin.

In late October C.S.M. Wigham, on a reconnaisance patrol from "A" Company to Hman Taung saw enemy on the track ahead of them.

Shots were exchanged but the Japs soon started their usual encircling tactics and the patrol had to withdraw. As a result of this brush, Lt. B. G. R. Stille was sent out with a strong patrol and though he found traces of the enemy, he was unable to locate them. He did however, contact a Gurkha Post from "V" Force, a semi irregular formation used for scouting and general ground intelligence work, which was operating in the area. On 1st November

Lt. R. A. F. Naylor on patrol to Namhkampat ran into five Japs at mile 14. A short skirmish took place which resulted in one Jap being killed. Two days Lt. Naylor again went down to Namhkampat but saw no enemy. Capt. Sheriff with a strong fighting patrol from "B" Company went beyond Namhkampat on November 7th and surprised and killed two Japs in a village North West of Mawlaik, which was occupied that evening by Lt. Stille's Platoon. Next morning they encountered a strong enemy position astride the track and after a short engagement withdrew to better ground. Before any more plans were made to deal with the Japs, contact was made with "B" Company 4 (U) K.A.R. who attacked and drove out the Japs, subsequently moving on to Mawlaik.

While all this was going on, a decision had been taken at Divisional Headquarters, that as soon as Mawlaik fell to the 21 (EA) Inf Brigade, the garrison at Letsegan should cross to the East Bank of the Chindwin and take over flank protection from the 1st Battalion The Assam Regiment. It was desirable that this force should have its own headquarters and as Headquarters 5 (K) K.A.R. now only had "D" Company under its command, Major W. D. Draffan, the second in command was sent off from Nyaungbin, with a small Headquarters Staff, to take over command and "Drafforce" was formed.

Major Draffan arrived at the Pt. 3069 position on the 10th November, 1944, having picked up on his way Lt. Keen, a new officer posted to the Battalion, Lt. Dixon, R.E., with a detachment of Engineers from 62 Field Park Company, and Capt. Miller of the Graves Commission. This last officer wished to register the graves of those killed and buried at Letsegan as a result of the action on the 22nd October, 1944.

The whole force was now put under the command of 21 (EA) Inf Brigade and Capt. Sheriff, still in the Namhkampat area having contacted Brigade Headquarters, sent back word that the remainder of the force was to concentrate at Mawlaik, collecting an air drop of rations at Thonhmwason on the way.

Lt. Dixon and the engineer detachment were at once sent forward to prepared the dropping zone at Thonhmwason and the next day Drafforce Headquarters with two sections from "A" Company followed. Major Barkas with the remainder of the force was left behind to collect a final air drop at point 3069 and follow on. Capt. Sheriff and an advance party had by now arrived at Mawlaik.

Unfortunately Signals got jumped and delayed, with the result that both the air drops at Point 3069 and Thonhmwason were cancelled without their knowledge. This caused an unnecessary hold up and left the force extremely hungry to say the least. However, the lack of food no doubt assisted them to get to Mawlaik all the quicker once they did start moving.

On November 13th O.C. Drafforce reported to Brigade Headquarters and received orders to cross the river as quickly as possible, take over from the Assam Regiment, and push down the East Bank so as to keep level with the 2 (Ny) K.A.R., who were thrusting down the West Bank.

The crossing started next morning, in rafts constructed of tarpaulin with bamboo strutted floors and with sides packed with grass. These rafts were paddled by six men and carried a further seven. There were also supposed to be able to carry one mule each. When loaded to capacity they were very low in the water and it was essential that everyone sat absolutely still to prevent accidents. Force Headquarters and "B" Company crossed first leaving "A" Company to see the rest over. At this point the river is about one thousand yards wide and it was necessary to pull the rafts some thousand yards upstream, embark and paddle furiously, but by the time the further bank had been reached, the raft had drifted at least half a mile downstream, and the whole process of towing upstream had to be done again before more passengers could be embarked. It was tedious and slow work, and the Engineers in charge of the rafts always seemed to want a great many infantry to repair them or make new ones. However, the troops got over fairly easily, it was the mules that caused the trouble.

In spite of many "experts" a satisfactory method of getting them across was not found and they had to be left behind. While trying to get them over a raft capsized in mid stream, causing the death of an askari. This man bumped into and was hit on the head by a small outboard motor boat which was cruising around in circles trying to rescue the occupants of the raft. His body was eventually recovered a mile downstream.

The crossing was not made any easier by the No. 11 wireless set being out of order. The original set brought down from Letsegan was at Brigade Headquarters for repairs, as the mule carrying it had fallen into a deep hole when crossing a chaung. A second set borrowed from Brigade Signals proved to be useless when tried out, and a third set taken over from the Assam Regiment was no better. This was not surprising as the Regiment said they themselves had been unable to contact Brigade and although Sgt. Pemble and the Divisional Signallers worked very hard over the sets they were unable to make them work and reluctantly came to the conclusion that there must be gremlins on them. This lack of wireless communication was infuriating as all messages for Brigade had to be sent back to the crossing place. Eventually they had to be swum over, not a very pleasant undertaking.

By the evening of the 15th Drafforce was ready to advance South. They had taken over from the 1st Bn. The Assam Regiment and established their Headquarters at Kyain, with "B" Company forward at Htanbingon. As it was still hoped to be able to get the mules over a rear party, under Lt. Naylor, (second in command of "A" Company), consisting of B Troop 101 Mortar Battery and the engineers were left behind to effect a crossing as best they could and follow on as quickly as possible. Arrangements for their rations were also made though it was expected they would very soon catch up the main body. It was a great misfortune having to leave the mules, which involved leaving the mortars as well, but it rendered the column more mobile: nor was there now a necessity to provide a guard for the mule train thereby reducing the effective strength of the companies. For transport the mules were replaced by local Burmese porters of all ages and both sexes. Twing did wonderful work organising them and altogether the force had a following of about seventy five. They worked without complaint and were never a worry. Whenever shots were heard they quietly hid in the jungle with their small guard and never once attempted to run away. They were paid with biscuits and small portions of other food but what they liked best was their ration of one eighth of a parachute per person per day.

This mobile force now consisted of:

    Drafforce Headquarters
    "A" and "B" Companies 5 (K) K.A.R.
    Detachment 5 (K) K.A.R. Signals Detachment II
      (EA) Division Signals.
    Detachment 2 (Z) Field Ambulance.

It soon found traces of the Japanese who appeared to be withdrawing a day or two ahead of it, and on the morning of the 17th a very early start was made. The general plan for the advance was to send forward as large a force as could be spared to occupy a commanding feature, while the remainder formed a firm base. As soon as the leading troops reached their objective the base moved up. Information of enemy positions and movements were badly wanted and the advantage of sending forward a strong advance guard was that no only were they able to brush aside small parties of enemy, but on arrival could send out patrols to either flank without seriously weakening their group. It was also hoped that extensive patrolling would deceive the enemy as to the true strength of the force. As the advance continued the difficulty of getting news back to Brigade Headquarters without a wireless increased but at least one message managed to get through each day. The first main bound was made to high ground North East of Ywatha which was considered to be about in line with the leading troops on the West Bank of the river. During a halt in the jungle at 08.00 hours the forward sentries of "A" Company saw movement. By silent signals the leading sections were deployed and in less time than it takes to write, Drafforce had its first prisoner. Fortunately he was not armed as otherwise it is doubtful if he could have been taken alive. The prisoner had swum the Chindwin during night, to escape our troops on the other bank and was quite exhausted. By mid-day Force Headquarters was at Hpatin and there met Lt. Peters of the Boat Section. This Boat Section had been formed to act as commandos and were doing a great job of work, going downstream by night and getting behind the enemy. They were a tough set of men, bristling with every sort of weapon imaginable, and were considerably annoyed to learn that for once they had been forestalled as they had intended to go to Ywatha themselves. However, it was a great stroke of luck meeting them as they took the prisoner and the useless wireless set back to Brigade Headquarters across the river. Capt. Culver, Staff Officer to Drafforce, was also sent over to give the Brigadier a personal account of what had happened to date and the force's future intentions.

"A" Company had by now occupied the high ground North East of Ywatha without opposition and the remainder of the force closed up on them. There they received the first news of enemy in any strength. Two tracks lead down to Ywatha village on the bank of the river. Lt. Seed and his platoon were sent along the more Northerly of the two, while Sgt. Mwangangi and his platoon went down the other. It was Sgt. Mwangangi who met the enemy and was forced to take up a position on some high ground between the two tracks. Sgt. Mwangangi then tried to get round behind the Japs but they proved too much for him and after a brisk action he withdrew. The enemy position held some thirty to forty men dug in but not in bunkers and from later information it was estimated that at least four of them were wounded in the fight.

While Sgt. Mwangangi was engaged Lt. Seed reached Ywatha without incident and sent a message back at 15.35 hours to say that he was looking for a place to set an ambush and had sent out a patrol to contact Sgt. Mwangangi. Nothing more was heard of him until next morning which caused a good deal of concern at Drafforce Headquarters. The trouble was caused through Lt. Seed's runner being unable to get back to him with orders from Headquarters, as he ran into Japs in the jungle and eventually had to spend the night out. Lt. Seed's patrol to contact Sgt. Mwangangi also failed to arrive for the same reason. The remainder of Drafforce spent an uneasy night knowing little of the enemy facing them and nothing of Lt. Seed's fate. To add to their worries at two in the morning, in the black of a moonless night, the sounds of a furious battle were heard from the direction of Ywatha and it was concluded that Lt. Seed's platoon was being attacked. The truth of the matter was that the Japanese were attacking the leading troops of the 2nd (Ny) K.A.R. who were on the other bank of the river opposite to Ywatha. During the evening Capt. Culver arrived back from Brigade with orders for Drafforce to push on so as to relieve the pressure in front of the 2 (Ny) K.A.R. on the West bank. On the following morning, having decided that there was insufficient knowledge of the enemy position to launch an attack, a strong ambush patrol was sent to establish itself astride the track south of the enemy. This patrol was lead by Sgt. Mwangangi as he knew that particular country. Meanwhile Capt. Sheriff with "B" Company less one platoon set off to test the enemy defences and gain what information he could preparatory to a full scale attack. The Japanese had however pulled out during the night and all that was found were a few remnants of clothing and signs of their wounded.

About the same time as the enemy position was reported clear, Lt. Seed returned to "A" Company with his platoon, having spent the night near Ywatha village.

The force having re-organised advanced in an endeavour to reach Tabagyaung; Lt. Armitage's platoon ("B" Company) leading followed by Force H.Q., and "A" Company. "B" Company less one platoon remaining as a base. At 13.00 hours Lt. Armitage's platoon which was still in the lead bumped eight Japs, wounding one and capturing five rifles and a good deal of equipment including a mail bag.

An hour later the same platoon, while moving along a ridge, saw a party of nine Japs in the valley below. They charged immediately but the Japs had too much lead and got away, but not before three of them had been wounded, leaving behind more stores and equipment. Lt. Armitage's platoon had one man wounded. Shortly after this encounter the largest hill in the vicinity was selected for a night bivouac, and the force struggled to the top and dug themselves in.

By now Drafforce was ahead of the troops on the West bank. Their advance had accomplished their object and the Japs fell back on the West bank, thus relieving the pressure on the Nyasalanders.

The next day was spent in patrolling forward and to the flanks. Capt. Warton with a platoon from "B" Company went to Tabguyaung and with orders from there to patrol to Welon where he was to reconnoitre forward as far as Masein and if possible set an ambush. This patrol accomplished its task and having had a look at Masein, which seemed clear of enemy, returned to base. Unfortunately a section from "B" Company sent forward during the afternoon to contact Capt. Warton and tell him to remain at Welon, so that the remainder of Drafforce could close up on him, took a different route through the jungle and missed him.

The second patrol also from "B" Company under Lt. Kleen was sent to Taung Tunhlaw and Nyaung-bin with orders to reconnoitre and set ambushes where possible. This patrol reached Taung Tunhlaw about three in the afternoon and were told by the villagers that a party of a dozen Japs were in position on feature Point 668. Lt. Kleen went forward with his section commanders, guides from the village, and an interpreter. According to the villagers the Japs were dug in at the foot of the hill presumably guarding the track which ran North and South on the eastern edge of the hill. There was a pagoda on the top of the hill from which a sentry could have had an excellent view of the surrounding paddy field which was approximately one hundreds yards wide. Altogether not a particularly inviting place to attack, Lt. Kleen decided to try and work his way up the western side of the hill unobserved from where he would have a good chance of surprising the enemy by attacking down hill. Corporal Wasso was detailed to cover the rest of the platoon across the paddy field, and immediately they reached the pagoda to move round the North end of the hill and come into action on the Japs' right flank. All went well and the attacking force crossed the paddy field unobserved and managed to get up to the pagoda although they had to crawl on hands and knees to do it. Half way round the side of the hill they were spotted and held up for a quarter of an hour by enemy fire and grenades. This delay allowed time for Corporal Wasso to come into action, and the enemy taken on both flanks fled before the determined assault of the two sections under Lt. Kleen. The interpreter posted as look-out at the Pagoda confirmed Corposal Wasso's estimate of thirty men, one of whom was being carried. Eight rifles, eighteen packs and a large quantity of food were found on the position. It was by now almost dark so having re-organised his platoon, Lt. Kleen returned to Taung Tunhlaw where the villagers rewarded him with an excellent meal. At eight o'clock that night the patrol started to return to base and, having spent the night in the jungle, joined up with Drafforce Headquarters at 9 o'clock on the morning of the 19th and handed in the captured arms and equipment. The work of this patrol has been given the prominence it deserved. From start to finish it was an extremely neat operation which might well serve as a model of this kind. As far as Drafforce was concerned their determined action removed a potential threat to its flank, and it must be one of the few occasions on which an African force routed an equal or large number of Japanese from dug in positions.

The third patrol under C.S.M. Wigham with four men from "A" Company went to reconnoitre a nearby dominating feature but returned to report no enemy in the area.

Next morning Drafforce again moved forward this time with the intention of reaching Balettha. By mid-day they were on a feature overlooking the river and Masein but it was decided that another hill to the East was more important and should be occupied and after another stiff climb they reached the top and started to dig in. This task was soon undertaken with the greatest vigour as shots were heard ahead of the foremost troops. This was due to a patrol under Lt. Armitage having bumped the Japs at the foot of the hill the force was occupying. It appeared that the enemy were covering a track junction, and in the exchange of shots one of our men was wounded. As a result of this Major Barkas left with two platoons of "A" Company to clear the enemy away from the hill, but found they had already withdrawn. "A" Company was however fired on from the other side of the river, when they moved into the open, and shots were gain exchanged. Two askari received wounds, and as the force had been ordered not to cross the river, they withdrew, leaving observation posts to watch the enemy.

During the afternoon enemy in ones and twos were seen moving towards Masein from the East. At 15.30 hours a a Forward Observation Officer from an Indian Light Battery joined Drafforce Headquarters and at 18.00 hours the same day Battalion Headquarters and "D" Company arrived, having crossed the Chindwin at Paluzawa.

PART V

Operations of "C" Company — November 1944.

On the 30th October "C" Company (Major G. L. G. Shaw) left Nyaungbin on an independent mission which lasted until the 10th December when they rejoined the Battalion in the Ingong Chaung.

The Company's first move was to Point 587, roughly half way between Nyaungbin and the main Yazagyo-Kalewa road. Here they came under command of the 26 (TT) K.A.R., a unit of the 25 (EA) Inf. Brigade and were given the task of protecting the Brigade's left flank from enemy infiltration from the East via the track Nyaungbin—Panma Taung. For the first week extensive patrolling was carried out, not only locally in the vicinity of Pt. 587 but South down the Bon Chaung to within a mile of the Kalewa Road. Amongst the most interesting of these patrols was one carried out by Lt. Becket who, when working in the Bon Chaung unknowingly slept within 150 of a party of Japanese, the first indication of what had happened being the discovery, when moving off next morning, of a camp fire still smouldering and empty tins of British rations, on which the Japs had partaken of their evening meal. Another was by Lt. Garside, who lead the patrol to the Kalewa road mentioned above, Lt. Garside unfortunately developed a poisoned foot, which slowed up his return journey, and resulted in his being evacuated to hospital. One of the most successful of all Patrols from Point 587 was one under the command of C.S.M. Hassan which got through to the road Kalemyo—Kalewa at a point to the West of the mouth of the Bon Chaung, where it remained for some time observing the Japanese activities in that area and returned bringing with it much information regarding Jap movements, transport, road conditions, etc., which proved to be of much value. The country on either side of the Bon Chaung made the going very difficult. It was all thick jungle and badly cut up with many small chaungs, tributaries of the main chaung, running between steep ridges which turned and twisted in every direction. From the information gained by this week of patrolling it seemed as if the Japanese were moving in small parties South and East from the main road above Kalemyo, using the small chaung leading to the Bon Chaung and thence along the main road to Kalewa. Although there was considerable activity on this stretch of road, mostly at night, there was no main highway in the Bon Chaung itself.

It was at this position that a mistake in a signal led to the whole of the Company evacuating its position and proceeding to 25 Bde. H.Q., a trek of about 15 miles through the most precipitous and dense jungle country, only to find on arrival that there had been a mistake and they had to return to Point 587 on the following day. On starting out on the return journey the Company was involved in an air attack by Japanese Oscar planes, on the 25 (EA) Bde. position but on account of the excellent cover which the jungle afforded from attack from the air, no casualties were sustained. On arrival at Point 587 an air battle between Oscars and our Dakota supply planes, was taking place over the area. One of the Dakotas was shot down and crashed in flames at a point which was estimated to be about three miles from Point 587. The whole Company to a man volunteered to form a search party to proceed to the aid of the crew of the crashed plane. From these a party of 15 men were selected and set out to endeavour to locate the plane, however, though the whole area where the plane was thought to be was searched. No trace of the plane or crew was to be found and unfortunately the attempt had to be abandoned. By this time darkness had fallen and the return journey was most eventful as the party completely failed for a time, to find its way through a myriad of chaungs and dense undergrowth, back to the main Chaung, which was their only possible guide to the Company position at Point 587. However, they eventually returned to their Company position about 20.00 hrs. mainly due to the almost uncanny sense of direction possessed by the African N.C.O's and askaris in this type of country.

The Company then under the command of the 26 (EA) Inf. Brigade was ordered to move South again as flank protection, to point 412 on the Bon Chaung, and from there to contact a company of the 4 (U) K.A.R., which were reported as being at Point 978, about two miles South West of "C" Company's position.

The move to Point 412 was through some very difficult country but was completed without incident and in good time, due mainly to the excellent guidance of Cpl. Monoiya and Pte. Kipto, who had been on patrol in that area with Lt. Garside. On arrival at Point 412, Lt. Coatswith was sent to make contact with the Uganda company at Point 978 only to find it occupied by the enemy. After a brief and inconclusive action, the patrol moved off towards the main road on the West and on their way found a telephone line which eventually led them to the Company they were looking for, but not before they again encountered some of the enemy.

Shortly after arrival at Point 412 Headquarters 4/4 (U) K.A.R. moved into the area and the Company was put under their direct command and given the task of finding out as much as possible about the enemy dispositions at the mouth of the Bon Chaung and on the Kalemyo—Kalewa road itself. The jungle hereabouts was denser than ever and gave such excellent cover that it was extremely difficult to know what was going on even in the immediate neighbourhood. On one occasion, C.S.M. Seymour, M.M., while on patrol to the Kalewa road located a Japanese camp only a quarter of a mile from "C" Company's position. There he saw Burmese working with elephants under Japanese direction, constructing a bridge. Hiding in the undergrowth the patrol watched Japs pass within forty yards of them quite unsuspecting their presence. The location of this camp however, must have been known to the Divisional Artillery, probably from aerial observation, for while it was still under observation by C.S.M. Seymour four shells landed in it.

On another occasion a patrol found a small party of Japanese complete with light automatic happily fishing in the chaung directly below the Company's camp. Needless to say they did not remain there very long after they were discovered. It would have been nice to be able to add that "C" Company dined on fish that night but unfortunately that was not the case.

A patrol to Pt. 1052 a high feature a mile to the East of the mouth of the Bon Chaung, found it to be occupied by about fifty Japs well dug in, in trenches and bunkers. As a result of this information the position was attacked from the air and engaged by the artillery. Reports now indicated that the enemy construction camp near the Kalewa road had been evacuated and Lt. Coatswith was sent to verify this information. He found it to be far from true, the camp being surrounded with sentries which indeed had not been the case previously.

"D" Company of the 4/4 (U) K.A.R. had, some little time before, been moved up to support "C" Company 5 (K) K.A.R. in their forward position and a provisional plan prepared for an attack on Pt. 1052 and the cutting of the road to Kalewa. It was then proposed to put this plan into operation but owing to rain causing delay in the general advance of the Division, the operation had to be postponed for four days, and the forward Companies withdrawn closer to Headquarters, 4/4 (U) K.A.R. This interim period before the attack was spent in close patrolling of the enemy position and the fixing of routes and assembly areas etc. On the day prior to the attack Lt. Becket was sent forward to make sure the enemy were still holding Pt. 1052, but had to make a hurried get away, without the required information, owing to the Artillery starting to range. On the 19th November this carefully planned operation was put into effect. "C" Company 5 (K) K.A.R. were to lead the assault on Pt. 1052, and on its capture, to move down and cut the Kalewa road. At 07.00 hours the Artillery concentrations came down on the enemy positions, and the infantry began moving forward until at 08.00 under cover of a mock air attack, the assault went in — only to find the position unoccupied. The mock air attack was designed to drive the Japs from their "Bunkers" as they were far easier to deal outside their "Bunkers" than when in them and it had been observed that when attacked from the air the Japs often preferred to evacuate their positions, take cover in the surrounding undergrowth and return to his bunker after the air attack was over. Without delay "C" Company swept down on the road which they cut and made secure at a point some four hundred yards East of Pt. 1052. Whilst moving along the Kalewa road the Company ran into a party of about thirty Japs and attacked immediately. The enemy thoroughly disorganized by this surprise attack lost seven dead and an unknown number wounded. Large dumps of stores were captured and a bridge blown up. Later in the morning the 4/4 (U) K.A.R. less one Company, joined up with "C" Company 5 (K) K.A.R. and a strong block across the road was established. The jungle around this block seemed to be alive with odd enemy snipers and small parties and great care was needed when moving about in this dangerous version of Blind Man's Buff. Major Shaw, himself no novice at the game, when carrying out a Recce for the positions to be taken up by the 4/4 (U) K.A.R., was preceded at a distance of about 2 yards by Pte. Nzioka, his Orderly, when a Jap leapt from the undergrowth and siezed Pte. Nzioka who rolled on the ground in a tussle with his assailant. Not being in possession of a Panga, for which Nzioka was shouting and not trusting the various tricks for which the Japanese were famous, Major Shaw shot the Jap dead as his Orderly struggled with him on the ground. For the next two days and nights this Guerilla Warfare went on, the Japs never leaving the position alone, shelling, sniping and mortaring, but never attacking in force. Naturally this activity encouraged the troops to dig themselves in properly with the result that only one man was killed and one wounded. During one night an enemy patrol of eight or ten men wormed their way into the Company's perimeter, and at dawn were seen in a small chaung. One was killed and one wounded before they escaped. Later in the morning the wounded man, whilst trying to slip out, was slain by Lance Corporal Shartugan using a Japanese sword which he had captured during the action on the road. On another occasion, Company Sergeant Major Hassan's platoon spotted a party of heavily camouflaged Japs in the distance. Hoping that they would come within point blank range, the platoon held its fire, but unfortunately the enemy turned off into the jungle. C.S.M. Hassan immediately ordered his Two Inch Mortar to open fire, with the result that a fighting patrol sent out under Lt. Becket, found one dead man in the area. The patrol failed to find the Japs who subsequently worked right round the Company's position and gave a great deal of trouble to the 4/4 (U) K.A.R.

Although these operations were the first serious fighting the Company had undertaken since entering the Kabaw valley three months before, the jungle conditions had taken their toll of British ranks, Lts. Garside and Joly and Company Quarter Master Sergeant Berkley all being evacuated sick at one time or another. Now the Company was to suffer another loss in Company Sergeant Major Seymour, M.M., who accidently shot himself, and also had to be sent to hospital. As these notes record C.S.M. Seymour had been doing some very valuable work and was a great loss to the Company which found itself seriously short of British Ranks. Nevertheless the African Ranks were an exceptionally fine lot of men and stepped nobly into the breech, C.S.M. Hassan being outstandingly good. Lance Corporal Pius Ochieng the Company's storeman although of humbler rank and appointment, also performed valiant deeds which the following episode well illustrates.

The road to Kalewa follows the North bank of the Myittha River turning South, at the mouth of the Bon Chaung, towards Kyaukka at which point it turns East again and enters the Myittha gorge. The Enemy were withdrawing Eastwards along this road, down which the Division was pressing, and putting up the most stubborn resistance in the high ground covering the entrance to the gorge. After the situation at the mouth of the Bon Chaung had been stabilised the Company were ordered to cross the Myittha and, by advancing along the South bank, get behind the Japanese positions on the North bank, thereby causing them to fall back. The crossing was carried out unopposed and Lance Corporal Ochieng, the Quarter Master Sergeant being in hospital, was left with a few men at the point of the crossing, to see that rations for the Company came forward. Owing to some mistake or other no rations were sent forward and Ochieng realising that something had to be done, stumped off to find Brigade Headquarters. There he refused to be put off by the usual bodyguard which surrounds Senior Staff Officers until he had seen the D.A.Q.M.G. himself and extracted the supplies he wanted. His next problem was to get them across the river and so quite undeterred he appropriated an assault craft and he and his merry men rowed them over. Thereafter they started humping the 180 lbs. bags of maize meal forward on their backs to where they expected to find the Company. However, the Company by this time getting hungry, had sent back a ration party which took over the job. Also before crossing the Myttha River, the Company left behind, in charge of L/Cpl Ochieng, certain company kit and stores. On hearing of this Bde. wished to take them over but L/Cpl. Ochieng refused to part with anything belonging to his Company.

The Battalion's Commanding Officer did not hear of this affair until long afterwards and promptly promoted Lance Corporal Ochieng Corporal—of the Battalion Headquarters Mess (Much to "C" Company's disgust) and subsequently to Sergeant Cook.

To assist in operations on the South bank of the Myittha a Company of the 13 (Ny) K.A.R. were placed under "C" Company 5 (K) K.A.R.'s command, and on the morning following the crossing the advance started, the first task being to clear Chaunggyin village of enemy snipers which were harassing the troops on the North bank. The village on arrival was empty of the enemy but their old positions were found and that night the force dug in on a precipitous hill overlooking the West end of the Myittha gorge and behind the flank of the enemy on the North bank. The jungle through which the Company had to pass on the advance to this village was by far the most difficult it had experienced during the whole of the Burma campaign, and to those who saw it it has always been a matter of wonder how the R.A. Signal Detachment, the Div. Signal Sec. and the L.M.G. crews got their equipment through it as they did. The Artillery forward Observation Officer with the Company found a good Observation Point and was able to direct accurate fire on the enemy's position, which the Company was also able to harass with small arms and light automatic fire. As a report was received that Chaunggyin village was again occupied by snipers, back went the Company, but only again to find it empty.

The next move was to Thitchauk village and to clear the high ground to the South. Lt. Coatswith went ahead with his platoon over the hills to the South, the remainder of the force following a little later, along the line of the river.

In a quick surprise attack on the village a party of Japs were routed and all their arms and equipment captured, amongst which were documents which proved to be plans for the defence of Thitchauk and for the withdrawal, together with further information giving the strength and dispositions for withdrawal to as far back as Kalewa. These documents were sent back to Brigade Headquarters, and although the messengers were sniped when crossing the river, delivered safely.

Major Shaw was subsequently complimented on his work on the South bank of the river and informed that the documents he had captured were the first that had ever been received in time to be of assistance to the Division in planning their attack.

In this action two Japs were killed and two wounded, "C" Company suffered no casualties. One of the dead was a Japanese Officer cut down by L/Cpl. Shartoyan using the Japanese sword he had captured previously bringing his successes with this weapon up to two. As a result he obtained a second sword of much finer quality from which he refused to be parted though one would have thought that the weapon with which he had killed his two opponents would have been of greater sentimental value.

On the heights above Thitchauk the Company was once again behind the enemy's flank and were able to send back information about his dispositions from which he was engaging the divisional armour. This resulted in accurate Artillery and Mortar concentrations being brought down, after which the Company engaged the enemy's rear with all possible fire.

The following morning the enemy position was found to be evacuated and a platoon under C.S.M. Hassan was sent forward to make the next bound along the South Bank. En route they met a party of Japanese and Burmese, and after a short quick skirmish, two of the Burmese were killed and two wounded, one of the latter being the pro-Japanese headman of a local village. "C" Company 5 (K)

K.A.R. were now told to hand over the advance on the South bank to the Company of the 13th (Ny) K.A.R. which up till then had been in their support and not actively engaged, and to cross back on to the North bank.

On the North Bank the Company had a few days well earned rest, and having found the Battalion Quartermaster with the Adminstration Company at Divisional Headquarters were able to get their mail and a few creature comforts. C.Q.M.S. Berkley rejoined the Company at this point.

Orders were now received for the Company to cross the Chindwin and rejoin 5 (K) K.A.R. operating with 21 (EA) Inf. Brigade on the East Bank. The crossing started at noon on the 5th December and was carried out in assault craft in three flights. The first flight came under shell fire, but this was inaccurate and caused no casualties. On reaching the East bank of the Chindwin the Company gave local protection to the 10th Field Ambulance for a couple of uneventful days. Then under command of 1 Northern Rhodesian Regiment they were ordered to proceed to 5 (K) K.A.R. by way of the Paung Chaung clearing it of any enemy in the process.

The move up the Paung Chaung was most nervous work. The Chaung ran through the thickest jungle in a deep ravine with, every now and then, sheer cliffs on either side. At places it was so narrow that only one man could move along the track at a time. Had the track been held or worse still the heights above, it would have been quite impossible to get through, and would have involved a detour of many miles through the most dreadful country. Fortunately this was not the case, and the Company eventually made contact with the 4th (U) K.A.R. at the Eastern end of the defile and were directed to the position held by the 5th (K) K.A.R. on the Ingon Chaung which they reached on the 10th December.

CHAPTER 10

BURMA — EAST OF THE CHINDWIN RIVER.

The force East of the Chindwin consisted of :—

5 (K) K.A.R. less Administration and "C" Companies.
B Troop 101 (Mortar) Battery R.A.
Forward Observation Officer and party from 2 Mountain Battery (3.7 Hows).
Detachment of 61 (Z) Field Ambulance.
Section 2004 Stretcher Bearer Company (Engineers?)

The task of this force was to keep the East bank clear of enemy while the remainder of 21 (EA) Inf. Brigade advanced South along the West Bank.

The whole force assembled in the Masein area and the enemy which had been confronting "Drafforce" withdrew. Lt. Seed with one platoon was sent down to Gazet and on to Kazet. At Kazet they surprised and routed a small enemy party in the village capturing rifles and stores amongst which was found an Officer's sword. As the rifles and stores were only a burden to the mobile force they were dumped in the river. A second patrol to Auktawgyi reported no enemy seen though local information indicated that small parties of Japs were still filtering southwards. The force then moved to Kazet and during the move captured a member of the Burmese Traitor Army and an old priest who was with him. During a halt Twing, who had been interrogating the prisoners, came in to report with a grin all over his face. It seemed that the Burmese traitor, who had been bound hand and foot, expecting to be killed at any moment had beseeched the priest to pray for his soul. However this the priest declined to do as he said he was far too busy praying for himself! The old priest was subsequently released as harmless.

On reaching Kazet "A" Company, who were in the lead found enemy in a gorge covering the only exit from the South end of the valley. As it was getting late the force dug themselves in on a high ridge some thousand yards West of the Japs, with the Chindwin, which at this point bends to the East, on their right and in front.

The Japanese were holding the high ground at each side of the rocky gorge, the entrance to which was not more than fifteen yards wide. They also held the high ground at its other end which later proved to be mined. Although there did not seem to be very many Japs holding the gorge they had to be cleared out to enable the force to move on down the river. Efforts to get round by the edge of the river failed as it was found that the cliffs fell sheer to the water, nor could any way up the cliffs on either side of the entrance to the gorge be found. To try and force the entrance itself would have been murder. Air support was therefore called on and the position attacked by twenty-four Hurri-bombers and bombarded with mortars but all this failed to dislodge the enemy. While waiting for the air-strike a patrol had been sent back to Auktawgyi to reconnoitre another track running across the ridge to Naungpanan behind the enemy's position and reported as being used by the enemy. This report proved correct as the patrol was fired on but received no casualties, so this route did not provide a ready made solution to the difficulty. It was therefore decided that the only feasible approach to the Kazet Gorge position was along the top of the ridge and "A" and "B" Companies with an R.A.P. were sent off during the night of 24/25th November to carry out this task. The plan was for "B" Company with the R.A.P. to form a base on top of the ridge astride the track to Naungpanan, while "A" Company moved South along the top to attack the Japs holding the gorge. The companies established themselves astride the track without difficulty and at 07.00 hours of the 25th "A" Company with one platoon "B" Company (Sgt. Brown) started moving South. The going was slow and difficult as the crest of the ridge was formed by a series of steep wooded pimple like hills and soon narrowed down to such an extent that only a section could be deployed. However, there was time enough to cover the distance to the gorge before the air strike which had been called for at two o'clock in the afternoon. The main difficulty was for the company to tell where they were on the ridge in relation to the gorge, but this was overcome by wireless communication with Battalion Headquarters. Every half hour or so Company Headquarters would halt and display a red umbrella (carried normally for ground to air identification) Battalion Headquarters who had a clear view of the ridge all the way down to the gorge. would then give them their location and directions for their next bound, when the process would be repeated until the Company finally arrived at their assembly area for the attack. Promptly at two o'clock the Hurri-bombers arrived and gave the enemy positions, indicated by a round of smoke from the mortars, an accurate bombing and straffing. As soon as the air attack was over "A" Company went in to find the position evacuated. It was characteristic of Japanese air defence methods to hide in the jungle away from their trenches during a "strafe".

If attacking troops could get there quick enough after the strafe there was a good chance of occupying the position before the Japs returned. On this occasion they did not return, which on the whole was just as well as "A" Company at first could only occupy the Northern edge of the Gorge, and would have had a difficult task capturing the other side. As soon as "A" Company reported themselves on the heights, "D" Company which had been lying in wait at the entrance for just this news went forward to complete the occupation, while the Fieldworks PPlatoon cleared up mines and booby traps. (The value of medium machine guns in jungle warfare has always been a debateable point but, here, and indeed in other positions later on, they could have been used with great effect. Curiously enough the cover provided by the jungle reversed the normal role of mortars and machine guns turning the former into a primarily defensive weapon and the latter into an offensive arm).

No time was wasted at Kazet and the following morning the advance, down the Chindwin, continued, led by "B" Company, the objective being the line of the Balet Chaung. The route fololwed an old telephone line and as the Battalion was now moving with the lie of the land the marching was not so difficult as hitherto, though one or two nasty patches of country were encountered. On arrival at the Balet Chaung "B" Company proceeded to dig themselves in on a narrow ridge between the river and the chaung and overlooking the villages of Myothit and Singaung. While the remainder of the force was moving along the east of the ridge, with the Balet Chaung on their left, and in front of them, a battle developed to the South East. African troops could be seen deploying over the flat ground beyond the chaung and "overs" from the battle were landing in and around the battalion column. At first it was thought that "B" Company were fighting a brisk action and the column was hurriedly halted, the mule train being pushed into the jungle for safety, while news was awaited. It turned out to be the 2 (Ny) K.A.R., (who were not expected in the area) clearing the Zidaw village. As soon as the situation became apparent the main body moved up onto the high ground immediately to the north of Myothit village and the Balet Chaung, a route being found for the mule train which did not expose it to the Nyasalanders battle on the plain below.

The situation was then as follows: The 2 (Ny) K.A.R. in the plains on the South side of the Balet Chaung and to the left front, were still fighting a spasmodic action. To the Bn.'s immediate front lay the Balet Chaung in a deep valley surrounded from the South by a horseshoe of hills, the highest Pt. 692 being roughly due South of the Battalion and some mile and a half distant. From Point 692 the hills swept around in a wide ridge, subsequently known as East Ridge, to the North East until they met the Balet Chaung. On the North West side of Point 692 they fell more rapidly to the banks of the Chindwin at their foot. In the centre of the valley so formed by this ring of hills lay the small but isolated feature of Myothit Hill with Myothit Village at its foot, and on the extreme right where the Balet Chaung joined the Chindwin was the large village of Singaung. The North bank of the Balet Chaung was for the most part a sheer cliff some hundred feet or more in height until the Chaung had passed through the valley into plainland on the East. This high ground was occupied by the 5 (K) K.A.R. with its right, "B" Company, overlooking the Chindwin and its left overlooking the plains.

Immediately this position had been occupied Lt. Clough's platoon from "D" Company were sent forward to investigate Myothit village and the high ground round Point 692. Myothit was found to be clear of enemy but no sooner had the platoon passed through Singaung than it came under fire from both Pt. 692 and the East Ridge, one man being killed. As soon as the platoon came under fire "B" Company on the right opened up in an effort to support them but almost immediately heavy explosions were heard in their area, to be followed by an irate and somewhat improper message from the Company Commander enquiring how the "something something" he was expected to give covering fire if the Battalion's "something" mortars would insist in shooting him up. Battalion Headquarters pained at both the tone and accusation of this message retorted that he was under fire from Japanese light mortars and advised him to do something about it.

"A" Company were then sent off to occupy East Ridge but bumped into an enemy position half way up, and as it was late in the day. started to dig in where they were. Darkness began to fall with the situation south of the Balet Chaung still far from clear so fresh dispositions for the night were made. "B" Company were withdrawn nearer to Battalion Headquarters and their position taken over by Battalion Headquarters Platoon under Lt. Senior, their task being to form a block on the ridge which in any event was too narrow for a full company, and prevent enemy infiltration from the right. "A" Company who reported their position as unsound and overlooked by an unknown number of the enemy were also withdrawn back to the North bank of the Balet Chaung, and a platoon of "D" Company under Lt. Cope sent forward to occupy the Myothit Hill which was regarded as a key feature.

The night brought forth no new developments and the following day was spent in proving the enemy positions and trying to pin-point his defence works. As it was thought that the main enemy force was around Pt. 692, "D" Company were ordered to drive off the enemy from the East ridge as a preliminary to a full scale attack on Pt. 692 at a later date. For this task they were given a platoon from "B" Company, to replace their platoon still on Myothit Hill, and were supported by "A" Company on a little hill just North of the main ridge. "D" Company managed to get close to the enemy position. The leading platoon under Lt. Clough was held up and Lt. Thomson's platoon trying to work round the flank also ran into a lot of trouble. The third platoon (Sgt. Brown) was then committed to try and force the issue but matters became too hot for them, the enemy being well dug in and in greater strength than supposed. Having obtained much accurate information as to enemy strength and dispositions the companies were ordered to withdraw. During the action Sgt. Brown and two askaris were wounded.

The failure to occupy East Ridge as planned was the first reverse the Battalion had suffered in Burma but the askari had their tails well up. "Bahati mbaya leo" said they "lakini kesho tutapigana tena".

During "D" Company's operation on East Ridge patrols had been sent to find out more about the enemy around Pt. 692 and the 3.7 Hows and our own Mortars had been ranging various targets, so by the evening it was possible to plan a full scale attack for the morrow. It was estimated that there were anything from sixty to one hundred Japs in the positions with the majority on the East Ridge. It was therefore planned that "D" Company should occupy Myothit Hill in strength and after an air strike, "B" Company passing through them were to capture Point 692 from the North East. "A" Company would engage East Ridge with small arms fire from the North, and on the fall of Point 692 East ridge would be captured by assault from the South West. This elaborate plan, involving as it did a number of changes in direction, had the great benefit that all troops taking part would be working on the arc of a circle, the centre of which was Battalion Headquarters position overlooking the Balet

Chaung and from which control of the operation would be easy.

On learning of the plan Brigade Headquarters, which had crossed the river at Masein, detailed units of the Brigade to block the tracks running South across the Japanese line of withdrawal, so that if all went well they would be unable to escape.

Battalion Headquarters in, as it were, the front row of the dress circle with the stage in perfect view below them felt very safe on the morning of the battle. The sun was shining from a clear blue sky and everything in the garden seemed lovely until the three inch mortar behind them misfired lobbing a bomb directly over their heads. Gone in an instant were jokes and laughter as with common accord they dived for the nearest trench, while fifty feet overhead the bomb, twisting and turning, began its downward decent to drop as luck would have it just clear of the cliff edge into the valley a hundred and fifty feet below. Capt. Clegg, the Mortar Officer was by no means popular with Headquarters Staff but as he also was forced to jump for cover and came in for his share of the ribald laughter that greeted Battalion Headquarters re-appearance above ground no more was said. At twelve noon the air strike by twelve Hurri-bombers started, the positions on Point 692 being accurately bombed and straffed. Despite indications given by smoke bombs from the Mortars, the aircraft ignored the positions on the East Ridge. This was most irritating as of the two positions East Ridges was considered the stronger. It was learnt later that the pilots could not see any positions from the air and therefore considered it a waste of ammunition. As the aircraft flew away "A" Company moved up onto the side of East Ridge, "D" Company deployed over the Myothit Hill from where they could cover both East Ridge and Point 692, while "B" Company passing through them commenced the advance to Point 692, their intended route being up the track between East Ridge and Pt. 692, thence swinging right handed onto Point 692 itself. Here the movement went wrong as "B" Company took a different track which eventually led them almost straight up on to Pt. 692, which they finally assaulted from the North. This loss of direction might have caused confusion to the plan as "B" Company were not sure where they were until they reached the high and open ground. Battalion Headquarters however could see what was happening, and being in good touch with all units were able to co-ordinate the movement. "B" Company's new line of advance was in fact shorter and they were able to occupy Pt. 692 unopposed, the enemy having evacuated their positions, probably as a result of the air strike. "B" Company now had the advantage of the high ground, and swinging back they swept down the hillside to the track which ran across the pass between them and East Ridge. During their advance they overtook a party of Japs who seemed to be making for East Ridge, killing three of them before they disappeared in the jungle, hurried along by a broadside from "D" Company on Myothit Hill. "B" Company made good the track and re-organised themselves for the advance North along East ridge, "D" Company being sent up to take over the track and support "B" Company's advance.

All these movements had taken time and it was close on five o'clock in the evening before "B" Company moving down the west side of East Ridge made contact with the enemy. "D" Company, leaving Lt. Clough and his platoon on the track, came in on a right hook on the East side and with "A" Company at the other end, the Japs were more or less surrounded. A fierce engagement in the thick jungle then took place, the Japs well dug in using small arms fire and grenades with great determination. In spite of energetic thrusts by all three companies it proved impossible to dislodge them and night came on before we could make use of the knowledge gained of the ground and the enemy defences.

This was a great disappointment as it was felt that another hour of daylight would have been sufficient to take the position. However, there was no use going on in the dark so "B" Company were told to dig in where they were in front of the Japs, "D" Company to withdraw to the track, and "A" Company, again at a disadvantage, to return home. During the action six dead Japs were counted and it was thought there must be many more on the East Ridge. Our own casualties had been almost miraculously light, only two askari being wounded the whole day.

Some very good work was done that night by the Company Quarter Masters of "B" and "D" Companies who got hot food forward in the dark to their companies despite the jungle and the proximity of the enemy.

During the day signal communication had as usual been excellent and Capt. R.T.M. Watson, second in command, of "D" Company from his vantage post on top of Myothit Hill had been able to keep Battalion Headquarters particularly well informed. On one occasion the Commanding Officer had an interesting and unusual experience. Whilst talking over a No. 48 set to Capt. Warton, second in command "B" Company, asking him how things were going, he heard the crack of a bullet in the earphones, followed by Capt. Warton's quite unperturbed reply that everything was going well "except that was rather a close one". As wireless communications even over short distances were pretty hopeless at night, telephone line was run out to the forward Companies. "B" Company having dug in close to the enemy and not knowing much about the ground spent a restless and anxious night, but the enemy activity which they heard proved to be a withdrawal, for in the morning their positions were empty. The 4 (U) K.A.R., who had been detailed to block the track south, later reported that a large party of Japs had burst through their line shortly before dawn. Unfortunately it had been a pitch black night with no visibility so they had not been able to stop them getting through.

In the morning "A" Company made a sweep through the whole area in case any enemy were still lurking about, and then the Battalion crossed the Balet and Kanni Chaungs to come into Brigade reserve and take over their protection and that of the 10th (z) Field Ambulance which gave all ranks a much needed rest for a few days.

During this short rest period the Battalion helped to make air strips on which small aircraft could land to evacuate the casualities. These strips were made in the dry paddy fields but never seemed to be right. In all, three strips were made before the pilots were satisfied. The 4 (U) K.A.R. were still sitting on a ridge between the Brigade's main line of advance and the Chindwin, and Lt. Thomson "D" Company was sent on a two day patrol to contact them in the area of Kywenan. Kywenan on the river was reached without incident but contact by wireless could not be made nor was it possible to scale the cliffs up from the river, so the patrol had to return. It transpired later the only way up the cliff was by ladder which had been removed either by the Japs or the locals. Meanwhile the (2 (Ny) K.A.R., were pushing forward until they were held up at Hmangon on the track South to Shwegyin. With a view to the future Lt. Armitage was sent forward to find a way round Hmangon to Point 752 which overlooked the track. The country was reported as very difficult with few tracks and once again against the grain of the country. However, Lt. Armitage successfully discovered a route to Pt. 752 and considering the difficulties of the terrain this patrol deserves special praise for the speed with which it accomplished its task. As the route required a good deal of work to make it passable for mules, "B" Company left at midnight on 2nd December 1944, being led by Lt. Armitage who had only had five hours rest since he came in, to open up the track for the remainder of the Battalion which followed seven hours later. By this time the Battalion had lost most of its following and had only its own troops plus the Forward Observation Officer from the Mountain Battery.

The Battalion arrived in the area of Pt. 752 without incident, but it was not long before patrols from "B" Company located enemy on the main track to the Ingon Chaung and Shwegyin, which ran through the valley below and to the West of Pt. 752. The country here was the most difficult yet encountered with innumerable hills and valleys so confusing that although we remained at Pt. 752 for three days we never really decided which was the peak itself. The enemy position on the track was equally difficult to pin point for though we had excellent observation over the valley and jungle below us, patrols returning found it extremely difficult to point out where they had been, and for one reason or another smoke bombs did not assist much. The enemy seemed to be moving about a great deal and using a 75 mm Infantry Gun with great cunning and persistence, firing mostly at the 2 (Ny) K.A.R. on our right rear, but always from a new position. In an endeavour to locate the enemy "A" Company moved to a position between Pt. 752 and the Ingon Chaung, where they were almost on top of the main track; but the Japs used it infrequently apparently keeping more to the West. "A" Company did however come across an Elephant chained to a tree. Ineffective efforts were made to release the brute and as Battalion Headquarters had not the heart to order its destruction there it remained. Undoubtedly the Japs subsequently used this animal to evacute their 75 mm gun, and it should have been shot but, well there it is . . . Capt. Warton and one section from "B" Company also put in some good work searching for the enemy and on one occasion had to spend a night uncomfortably close to a large party which decided to camp beside them. The Japs at this stage probably knew very little of their own dispositions or they would not have been wandering about in the jungle in the way they did.

From Pt. 752 Capt. Valentine, the Intelligence Officer, patrolled down to the Ingon Chaung to find a position into which Brigade Headquarters could eventually move and where a dropping Zone could be made. Having crossed the Chaung and started to climb the ridge on the further side he heard noises in the chaung and on looking back saw a meeting taking place in the Chaung between a Japanese officer and men, the officer having ridden up the chaung from the East mounted on a white charger. After a short conference the Japs spotted Capt. Valentine's footprints and set off to look for him, however, he easily evaded them in the jungle. This and other patrols showed that there was much enemy activity in the valley of the Ingon Chaung, the Japanese moving South mostly by night using the river beds and avoiding the tracks. Under these circumstances the Bn. was unable to set any effective ambushes. Meanwhile Lt. Clough with a platoon from "D" Company were sent to test the strength of the only known position astride the Shwegyin track, and by a surprise attack successfully routed the enemy in a short sharp action in which one of them was killed and one askari wounded. The Japs however, soon recovered from their surprise and being in superior numbers started to encircle the platoon which then withdrew. This position which had proved so hard to locate was never attacked in strength, as the Battalion was ordered to by pass it and move South to secure a base for the Brigade on the Ingon Chaung. There was however an Air Strike on it on the 6th December by six Hurri-bombers which was thought to be very successful, at any rate it had the desired effect as on the 8th December it yas found to be evacuted.

"A" and "B" Companies were the first to move to the proposed base on the Ingon Chaung but not before the Japs again shelled the Bn. with their infernal 75 mm gun. All their shots however, fell wide and did no damage. At this new base arrangements were put in hand for the reception of the Brigade Units and the construction of a Dropping Zone which involved the felling of a large number of trees along the edge of the chaung. This was a busy time as besides these activities a sharp watch had to be kept on the enemy who popped up like Jack-in-the-box in all directions, and there was little rest for anyone. A long distance Patrol under Lt. Kleen to Point 933, a hill at the head of the Ingon Chaung, had an arduous journey and although they found old tracks and traces of the enemy, did not meet any. Another patrol under Company Sergeant Major Chilcott with a sergeant of Engineers was sent to have a look at the main road which the Japanese were using for their withdrawal from Kalewa. Their main task was to find a route passable to mules to the stretch of road between Mutaik and Chaungzon, with a view to mining the road and setting an ambush. This patrol which took two days reported they could find no route for mules but the main road was ideal for mining and ambush, and they had heard enemy lorries moving on it during the night. As a result Lt. Lawrence with his platoon from "A" Company and an engineer detachment under the same sergeant were, a little later, sent to lay the mines. They arrived just at dusk and saw fresh wheel marks on a well worn track and soon spotted a Japanese sentry nearby. The patrol laid up for a little and eventually started to lay the mines at eleven o'clock by the light of the moon. Three lorries were heard moving but all stopped short of the minefield: later on a large party of the enemy passed by some distance away and it was thought that some of them left in one of the vehicles. Nothing however, came over the minefield. In daylight next morning it was realised that the mines had been laid on a side road leading to a dump, which seemed to have been cleared only the day before, and not on the main road at all. This was most unfortunate but as the patrol had been ordered not to delay their return there was nothing for it but to leave the mines where they and hope that the track would be used again.

A very successful patrol was carried out by Corporal Jilalo of "B" Company, down the Ingon Chaung to Ingon village, and thence to the main road and Mutaik. This entirely African patrol, on its return, reported approximately one hundred Japs at Ingon village, and enemy transport on the main road. Great credit is due to this African corporal for his excellent report which proved to be accurate and of great value.

At this time there were so many patrols and ambushes organised that it is not possible to record them all.

An important patrol under Lt. Robertson "A" Company was detailed to open the track from the Ingon Chaung to the Gonga Chaung but ran into an enemy position at the point where the track met the Ingon Chaung a little to the west of the Brigade base. Lt. Robertson engaged the enemy but finding them dug in returned, having gained much useful information. Meanwhile a platoon under Lt. Senior operating as a fighting patrol ran into more Japs the same evening. Having observed the enemy without being seen themselves they quickly set an ambush. Holding their fire until the enemy were within twenty yards they killed two and wounded others, L/Cpl. Lomgeti's section taking the initiative. The Japs then appeared in force and Lt. Senior withdrew.

As the Jap position on the Ingon Chaung was much too close to the Brigade Base to be comfortable, "A" Company were detailed the following day to see what could be done about it. The Japs however were too well dug in to be intimidated by one company and opened up with all they had. During the action Lt. Robertson was mortally wounded and three askari less seriously so. This caused a set back in the plan of attack though Sgt. Mwangangi immediately took over command of the platoon and managed to get Lt. Robertson back. He died of his wounds before he could be taken to the Regimental Aid Post. After inflicting casualties on the enemy but not being able to dislodge them the company withdrew. This position had now to be given serious attention and an air strike on it was arranged for the afternoon of the 8th December. "B" Company with Sgt. Mwangangi's platoon from "A" Company and Sgt. Gethi's platoon from Battalion Headquarters were detailed for the attack and moved down to the position occupied by "A" Company in the previous day's abortive action, from where Capt. Sheriff Commanding "B" Company made his recconnaisance. At half past four in the afternoon the air strike came in followed by a fifteen minute concentration from the Mountain Battery, and as the last salvoes fell the Company moved into the attack. The first position was surprised and rushed, two Japs being killed and much equipment, including ammunition for the 75 mm gun, captured. The Company then went on to clear up a second position which they found on a spire-like peak above them. The enemy opened up with everything they had and managed to slow up the attack, until in the failing light, when within thirty yards of the enemy trenches, Capt. Sheriff, after referring to Battalion Headquarters, was directed to break off the engagement. Here again the late hour of the air strike, over which Battalion Headquarters had no control, left insufficient time for completion of the assault before dark, and the idea began to formulate as to whether in future it would not be better to dispense with air support and so be able to start earlier in the day.

That night the company remained close up to the enemy and in the morning recconnaisance patrols reported the position evacuated. During the action L/Cpl. Mbuli had been killed and Capt. Sherriff and two askaris wounded. The enemy casualties were not known. Capt. Sherriff, although wounded in the arm, remained in command of the Company until the action was over, when he allowed himself to be evacuated to hospital and handed over command to Capt. Warton who remained in command of the Company until the end of the Battalion's operations on the Chindwin.

During "B" Company's attack, to add to the excitement, the Japs opened up with the 75 mm gun on the Brigade Base but inflicted no casualties.

The Brigade was now given the task of cutting the main road in the Sizwe — Chaungzon area to form the eastern side of the Divisional Brigehead around Kalewa. To accomplish this task the Brigadier ordered 5(K) K.A.R. forward to find and form a hidden base close to the main road from which Brigade units could be secretly deployed to cut the road in one movement. Early on the morning of the 9th December the Battalion moved out following the general line taken by the mine laying party. As no mules could be taken the troops were heavily laden with ammunition and rations which made the going over the most impossible country extra difficult. At one point the column found itself faced with a sheer bluff fifty or sixty feet high, and for sometime no way round or up it could be found. However, after working with pangas the troops managed to make a track of sorts, up which they could just crawl. Eventually the Battalion arrived at a shallow depression just behind a ridge a mile from the main road, and as this appeared suitable to the purpose, camp was made although at that time the exact locality was unknown. As secrecy was essential to the task no patrols were sent out except to verify the location of the main road and to find an easier way up the bluff for the Brigade Units that were to follow the next day.

That evening the Commanding Officer spoke to the Brigadier over the wireless and was informed that the Japanese had been shelling the Ingon Chaung, one shell landing accurately in the dug out in which the Commanding Officer had been living for the last three days. That night, as the Bn. lay in its secret base listening to the whine of heavy shells passing overhead in an Artillery duel, it was hoped that neither side would be tempted to shorten their range.

Next day the Brigade Units arrived and tagging along behind to our great joy came "C" Company fresh from their wanderings in the Myittha Gorge. 2 (Ny) K.A.R. who had been detailed to cut the road next morning passed straight through the camp to lie up for the night within a few hundred yards of their objective., the Battalion assisting them to carry forward the stores they needed for their operation. Next morning the road having been cut without incident the Battalion less "C" and "H.Q." Companies moved up to support the 2 (Ny) K.A.R. in case of counter attack by the enemy. Lt. Armitage with his platoon from "B" Company was sent on patrol up the Ingyingaing Chaung and ran into a party of the enemy just before dusk. In a sharp short action at least one of the enemy was killed and an askari and Lt. Armitage wounded. As the enemy were in superior numbers and, as usual, started their encircling tactics, the action was broken off and the patrol withdrew. Both Lt. Armitage and the askari were in great pain from their wounds but since the country was so broken that it was inadvisable to attempt to return by night they camped not far from the scene of the action and sent back runners for the Medical Officer and stretcher bearers. Although in possession of morphia Lt. Armitage, with great devotion to duty, refused to use it upon himself feeling that under the prevailing circumstances he must remain alert during the night.

Meanwhile "B" Company were sent forward to a position overlooking the road from the North and well in front of the 2 (Ny) K.A.R. position and there reported a body of the enemy digging in some four hundred yards south west. Other parties of the enemy were heard moving westwards through the Jungle but it was seldom possible to catch more than a glimpse of them so "B" Company had to content themselves with spraying the area with automatic fire and two inch mortar bombs. The Battalion was now detailed to take a left hook through the jungle with the object of getting behind the enemy opposing "B" Company and opposite Chaungzon which was reported as a large enemy camp still containing a few Japanese, including a detachment of "Geisha girls". The jungle in this area was the worst yet encountered, the land not seeming to conform to any pattern with the chaungs and ridges running in all directions. It was, however possible to get a number of view points but even from these it was found difficult to locate points with any accuracy. Eventually the assistance of the artillery flying Observation Post was called for by putting up the red umbrellas as the aircraft came over. The navigator then gave the Battalion position by wireless and inevitably it was found to be at least half a mile from where it was estimated the troops always having covered less ground than imagined.

As the Battalion closed on Chaungzon from the North "C" Company whilst crossing the Ingyingaung Chaung came under fire, one askari being wounded. The enemy were however routed and their position on the opposite bank occupied. Continuing their sweep "C" Company again met the enemy and a brisk running fight took place, the enemy adopting guerilla tactics. The area was quickly cleared eight of the enemy being killed and at least seven wounded. "C" Company's casualties amounted to five wounded, including L/Cpl. Shartuyan, he of the Sword, which made this askari very cross. "I must be going blind" said this cheerful warrior "for I certainly should have seen and killed him before he saw me". Subsequently Shartuyan had to be evacuated to hospital still grasping his beloved Sword and furnished with a letter from the Brigadier threatening the direst penalties on anyone in the back area who tried to part him from it. Eventually East Africa Command learning the story made special arrangements for the safe custody of the sword which was sent to Shartuyan's District Commissioner and formally handed back to him after his discharge from the army. It was Shartuyan's professed intention to use this weapon for herding his cattle after the war if indeed he carried out his intention it seems an ignominious end for a Samurai's sword.

Meanwhile "A" Company were sent across the Chaung to establish a block on the road and shortly afterwards reported themselves in a position "sawa sawa Gibralta" which seemed satisfactory. Patrols were now sent in to the Japanese camp itself which proved to be a large rambling affair many hundreds of yards wide, and one more enemy was found and killed. Although evidence of females being in the camp were found, no "Geishas" were captured. Next morning the remainder of the Battalion, which had spent the night on the West bank of the Ingyingaing Chaung, crossed over together with the mule transport which had now come up, and the Battalion's final dispositions in Chaungzon area were taken up on the 16th December 1944. The road back to Kalewa was now clear of the enemy and all troops were thankful to see the Battalion Jeeps arrive bringing with them a certain amount of spare kit of which all stood in need.

On the 17th December the Battalion was honoured by a visit from the Divisional Commander, General C.C. Fowkes, who talked with all ranks and had a cup of tea in the Mess. It was here that the Signal Officer completed his last miracle. The General wished to talk to his Headquarters with whom he had been out of touch for the last twenty-four hours. So for that matter had our own signals but without batting an eye-lid the Signal Officer replied "Very good Sir" and went off in fear and trembling. However to his amazement Divisional Headquarters came through clear and distinct. "Ha, knew I could trust the fifth" said the General as he went off to speak. Ten minutes after he had finished the set went off again and remained so for the rest of the day.

The Battalion remained at Chaungzon for a week carrying out various patrols locally and down the road towards

Ye-U. On only one occasion were any enemy encountered which resulted in a few shots being exchanged but no casualties on either side.

With the formation of the bridge head round Kalewa the divisional task was completed, and the 2 British Division passed through to continue the advance to the Irrawaddy.

On December 23rd the Battalion pulled out marching back to Shwegyin where it was interesting to see the tanks and other equipment left by the British forces during the evacuation. At Shwegyin all troops embarked in "ducks" and were taken upstream to Kalewa where the famous Bailey Bridge built by the engineers and reputed to be the longest of its kind in the world was crossed. As the Battalion was leaving Kalewa in Motor Transport bound for Indaingale the Japs sent over a final "Kwa Heri" of bombing the bridge unsuccessfully. At Indaingale the Battalion spent Christmas, and there it learnt the very sad news that General Fowkes was to leave the Division due to ill health, the Divisional Commander's farewell letter is attached as an Appendix. After Christmas evacuation by air to Imphal was carried out. This evacuation was a strange affair. Having been warned that just so many troops and so much stores could be taken by each aircraft the Battalion spent hours working out loads and parties. However when the aircraft came in the pilots had other ideas, some taking far more, these were generally the Americans, and some far less. As the aircraft never landed twice in the same place the aerodrome was soon filled with small bodies of Africans doubling about from one machine to another. However all got off some how, the Africans, who had never flown before, being totally unconcerned over this new way of travel. From Imphal the Battalion left in trucks driven by Indian Army Services Corps drivers, down a fearsome road twisting through the hills and boarding a steep ravine for the most part. After this experience our opinion of the African Driver rose immensely. Finally it reached an area just North of Dimapur where the Division was concentrating for a rest and refit.

Although it was not known at the time the Battalion had seen the last of Burma.

CHAPTER 4.

ASSAM AND BENGAL — JANUARY — AUGUST 1945

At Dimapur the Battalion was fortunate enough to be given one of the best camp sites on the banks of a gently flowing river with its back to a patch of forest.

Knowing that it would be there some little time great care was taken with the lay out of the camp, the first few days being spent in temporary accommodation while proper quarters were built on carefully chosen sites. Being accustomed in Africa and Burma to cut what timber was needed for building and firewood the Askaries used the patch of forest for this purpose. Fortunately most of the requirements had been extracted before orders were received to stop immediately, the forest being the property of the locals who were demanding enormous compensation.

For the first few weeks very little attention was given to training, the majority of working hours being spent in smartening up the Battalion on the parade ground and improving the camp.

The troops welfare was catered for with many Ngomas and there being an adequate supply of local native beer these were a great success. Crime was negligible though one or two cases did come before the Commanding Officer. Apparently the punishments awarded were too light for he was severely reprimanded by his Nandi orderly who said that he and his brother Nandi had been talking the matter over and he had been deputed to inform the Commanding Officer that offenders should be soundly beaten and "What's more" he added 'you ought to rub in salt afterwards like the District commissioner does". Unfortunately regulations did not permit of this advice being accepted.

Meanwhile the British ranks were organising several long delayed Christmas parties amongst the more successful of which was a "Garden Party" given by the Battalion and attended by the new Divisional Commander, Major General Mansergh.

While at Dimapur the Battalion was inspected by the Army Commander, General Sir William Slim, who presented medal ribbons to personnel of the Battalion awarded decorations. (Lt. Col. T. C. C. Lewin, the Military Cross. Sgt. E. C. J. Bull, Corporal Chelalo Gapo, Corporal Mohamed Aden, the Military Medal.) At the conclusion of the parade the Army Commander gave an address to the Battalion, extracts from which are included in the Appendices.

As it was hard to find suitable places to which the askari could go on leave, special leave camps were arranged.

The idea of these was at first unpopular but after a few men had been persuaded to try them out they became very popular and everyone wanted to go.

The weather began to turn cold but all ranks were well supplied with blankets and the change from the heat of the jungle was very welcome. As the rainy season approached the Division had to move out and in early Spring concentrated at Chas some thirty miles from Ranchi.

Chas was quite the most horrible place in which the Battalion was ever stationed. Situated in the coal mining area of Northern Bengal it had no redeeming features and was reputed to be used normally as a "Penal Station". There was practically no cover and troops lived under canvas. Every few days there was a dust storm which blew the tents down and as these storms were almost inevitably followed by a thunder storm everything got soaked. Gradually the weather grew hotter and hotter until all were roasting in a normal daily shade temperature of between 116 and 120 degrees Fahrenheit. The whole camp area was almost completely bare of vegetation and a magnificant example of sheet erosion. This was not at all surprising because as soon as a few blades of grass did appear the local natives came out and dug them up before anyone else get them. These locals were pretty miserable people who even had to keep the wheels of their bullock carts locked in their houses in case a neighbour should steal them during the night. Despite these unpleasent conditions the Battalion got in a lot of useful field training exercises, some independently and others in co-operation with other units.

Just when the troops began to feel they could stick Chas no longer the welcome news of a move to Ranchi plateau was received. This was very much better and the Battalion settled down to serious training for its new role which it was understood would be second flight troops to expand and hold a beach head after an initial assault landing "somewhere in South East Asia". But soon the war in Europe was over and under the terms of age and service many of the British ranks of the Division were due and overdue for release. As it was not possible to replace these before the Division was required to go into action Commanding Officers were asked to ascertain how many would be willing to postpone release for six months. As far as the Battalion was concerned there were very few who did not voluntarily agree.

As many raw reinforcements had arrived in the Battalion a battle inoculation scheme was devised to condition them to heavy gunfire. While making their reconnaissance for this scheme the Commanding Officer, Second in Command and one Coy Commander were very nearly eliminated by an Indian 5.5 Battery opening up on the area although it had been allotted to 5 (K) K.A.R. for the day. They didn't seem to mind very much at Division remarking that sort of thing was often happening.

August 1945, with the dropping of the Atomic Bomb at Hiroshima and the Japanese surrender, found the Battalion still in training at Ranchi.

In a moving little service conducted by Padre, Father Harry, the Battalion gave thanks to God for His mercies.

THE END.

APPENDIX 4.

OFFICERS COMMANDING 5 K.A.R.

1902	Maj. M. L. Hornby, D.S.O.
1916 — 1918	Lt. Col. W. E. H. Barrett.
1919	Lt. Col. J. M. Llewellyn.
1920	Major G. C. Hill.
1921 — 1923	Lt. Col. J. M. Llewellyn.
1924	Lt. Col. T. S. Muirhead.
1924	Major W. V. D. Dickinson.
1925 — 1926	Lt. Col. T. S. Muirhead.
1930 — 1934	Major J. R. Guild.
1935 — 1936	Major W. H. Rowe.
1937 — 1940	Lt. Col. T. L. Barkas.
1940	Lt. Col. J. H. de la Herapath.
1941	Lt. Col. J. R. H. Dowling.
1941	Lt. Col. R. A. F. Hurt, D.S.O.
1942	Major H. D. Tweedie.
1942	Lt. Col. P. A. Morcombe, O.B.E.
1944	Lt. Col. T. C. C. Lewin, O.B.E., M.C.
1945	Lt. Col. W. D. Draffan, M.B.E.

APPENDIX 1.

ADJUTANT'S BATTLE LOG.

(LETSEGAN). 22nd **October 1944.**

0830 Air strike on Pt. 3069 by 12 Hurribombers commenced.
0920 101 Mortar Battery reported enemy patrol strength unknown fifty yards South of their position and have sent out own patrol to engage.
0925 Battery report enemy patrol moved off.
"B" Company reported to have reached point where tree had fallen across the track.
0930 Battery request permission to range on Pt. 3069.
0932 Line to Battery "DIS".
1010 "B" Company reported moving up to objective.
1012 Battery given permission to range on Pt. 3069.
1020 Battery report not ranging on Pt. 3069 because of "B" Company moving up.
1022 "B" Company informed battery not ranging.
1035 Enemy small arms open fire on "B" Company Adforce Headquarters and "D" Company reported in position.
1037 Battery concentration on enemy position comes down.
1038 "D" Company moving up to first objective.
1040 "B" Company attacking their objective.
1042 "D" Company report battery concentration falling on target No news of "A" Company but "D" Company report that they can hear firing from "A" Company's flank.
Enemy fire on "D" Company.
1043 "D" Company 4/4 (U) K.A.R. shot one sniper in rear of Adforce.
1057 Adforce Headquarters moved up 500 yards.
1108 "D" Company engaging small O.Ps. of 3069 feature.
1110 "B" Company report some casualties including Major R. P. Townley and Lt. Cheyne wounded.
1112 Still out of touch with "A" Company.
1115 C.O's. Command Post moves forward to original Adforce Headquarters site.
1135 Adforce Headquarters move to Bashas.
1150 "D" Company left hand Pl. held up by automatic fire O.C. "D" Company moving right hand Pl. round flank.
1155 "B" Company report casualties considerable, unable to move forward.
1159 "A" Company held up 50 yds. inside first wire, casualties heavy caused by snipers, L.M.Gs and grenades.
1205 "A" Company walking wounded arrive at R.A.P.
1210 "B" Company still held up inside the wire but will attack when Adforce open up again.
1223 "A" Company evacuating casualties 300 yards behind their position in Chaung.

1225	Right flanking Platoon of "D" Company held up but have contacted "A" Company. "D" Company moving reserve platoon round the left.
1227	"D" Company casualties, two leg wounds caused by grenades.
1240	One Platoon "D" Company 4/4 (U) K.A.R. left to go under Command Adforce.
1254	"D" Company getting in round left flank.
1300	Adforce report "D" Company made first objective Pt. 3069.
1305	"B" Company ordered to withdraw to R.V. Second Platoon of "D" Company 4/4 K.A.R. sent to Adforce to assist in making secure.
1310	Adforce ordered to dig in and prepare for counter attack.
1330	Sent up reserve ammunition C.O. and I.O. Move to Pt. 3069.
1355	Walking wounded left for Letsegan.
1400	"D" Company report 17 casualties wounded.
1420	"A" Company report 47 casualties including C.S.M. Raguti killed.
1425	"B" Company report concentrated at R.V. sent out patrol to find way round right flank.
1430	Command Post moves to Pt. 3069 with remainder of "D" Company 4/4 (U) K.A.R. "B" Company ordered to drop one platoon as stop reminder to move to Pt. 3069 as force reserve. "D" Company 4/4 (U) and "D" Company 5(K) K.A.R. taking up covering position forward of Pt. 3069.
1445	Patrol reports one enemy bunker evacuated.
1450	"D" Company 4/4 (U) K.A.R. ordered to advance and mop up.
1515	Lt. Scott "D" Company 4/4 (U) K.A.R. reported his patrol have occupied deserted bunker West of Pt. 3069.
1525	C.O. reconnoitres enemy position West of Pt. 3069.
1530	"B" Company arrives at Pt. 3069.
1535	C.O. reports enemy have run away and position now ours.

APPENDIX 2.

EXTRACTS FROM ARMY COMMANDER'S ADDRESS AT DIMAPUR, JAN. 1945.

"I have not been able to see as much of the 11th East African Division as I would have liked. I have visited several of your Units in action in the Kalewa area. I always like to get to know as well as I can the men under me, but an army is a very large force, and I cannot meet you all as often or as intimately as I would wish. However if I cannot get to know you personally I think it is a good thing that you should know me, so take a good look at me. Then when you see me about the place you will know that I 'Belong'. Besides one of the things that I disliked more than anything else when I was a more Junior Officer than I am now was being ordered about by a fellow I had never seen. Well now you've seen me. We in the 14th Army in the last year have fought a very successful campaign. Around Imphal we gave the Japs the biggest thrashing he has ever had and got him on the run. If you get your enemy on the run, the thing to do is to get after him and give him no time to get his breath and reorganise. That is why it was so important that we should follow him up. I had been told by a lot of people that it was impossible to operate in the Monsoon. However, I had done two Monsoons myself, and I was sure that really good troops would be able to move and fight in the appalling conditions of Monsoon and that it where you came in. I asked you to do it and you did it. Let me tell you there are very few divisions in the world who could have done what you and the Fifth Indian Division did. You carried out every task that was set you, including the establishment of a bridge head across the Chindwin, and those troops of the 14th Army now advancing into Burma are reaping the benefit of what you did. Every man who was in the 11th East African Division can be very proud of the 14th Army's victory, and I want personally to say "Thank you" for you contribution to success. We have given the Japs a real hiding, but he is a tough little insect as you know, stupid but tough. He is fighting back and going to put up a tough struggle for Mandalay. This means that before Burma is clear, there is a great deal of fighting ahead and for that your Division will be required again. You now have the opportunity of training for the next round. You know your weak points. Every Division in the world has its weak points, and knowing them is the first step to curing them.

Where you find yourself now may not be the place where you would most like to be, but it is the best I have been able to find for you, and I believe it is a great deal better than many. I have put you all on convalescent rations. As a matter of fact you don't look very delicate, but I won't tell the Doctors that. I hope while you are here, you may also have an opportunity of leave, and I am trying to improve leave centres for both Europeans and African Ranks.

APPENDIX 3.

DIVISIONAL COMMANDER'S FAREWELL LETTER

11 (EA) Div.

28th Dec. 1944.

1. The time has arrived when higher authority has decided that I must be considered war weary and no longer physically fit to command an operational formation. I do not of course, agree with them but as you well know there is no appeal, and anyway new blood does no division any harm.

2. I am not issuing any farewell order or message either to British or African ranks because to do so might give the impression that I was leaving owing to the shortcomings of the Division at a moment when everyone is justly proud of the successful campaign we have completed. The opposite, indeed, is the case and I have had many messages from the Supreme Commander downwards congratulating the Division on its success. These letters of congratulation will be published in the usual way.

3. Now let me thank you for the loyal support you have given me both in raising and training the Division and leading it to Victory. We have had bad times as well as good times, but I only hope you have enjoyed it as much as I have. My hopes and prayers will lie with the Division for as long as it is in Burma, and I am fully confident that it will continue to add to the high prestige it has already won.

Yours sincerely,

C. C. FOWKES.

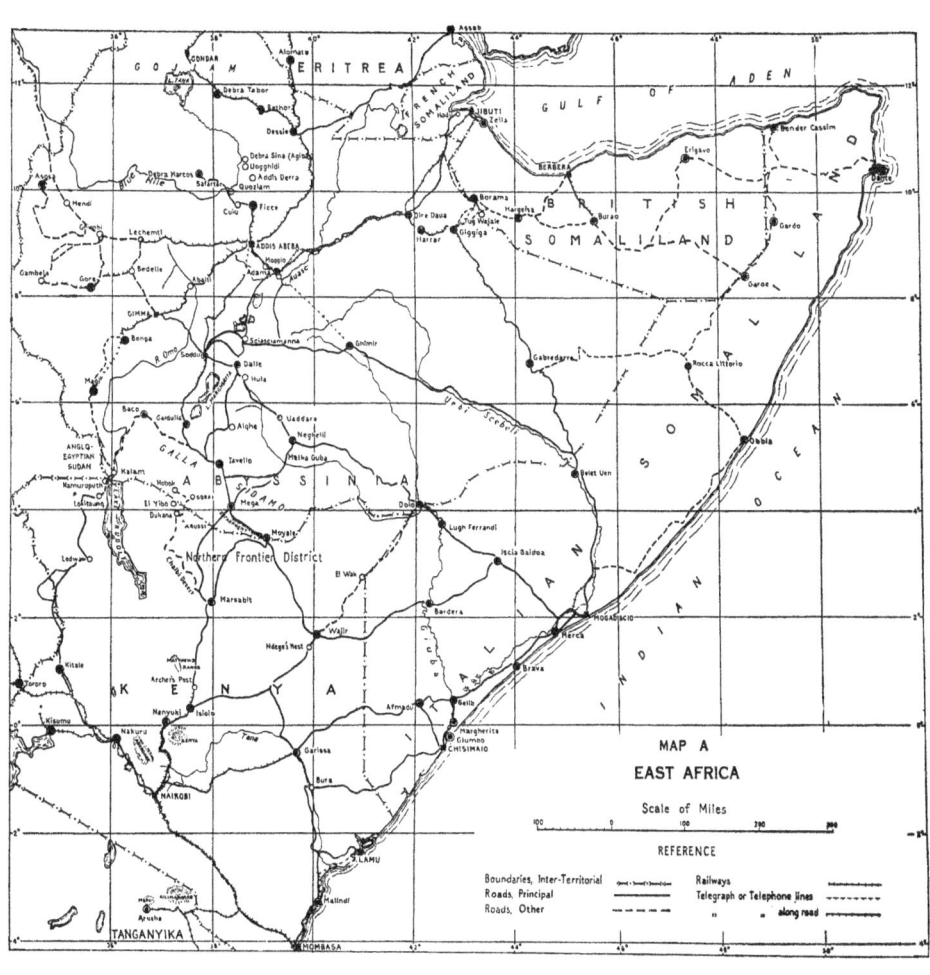

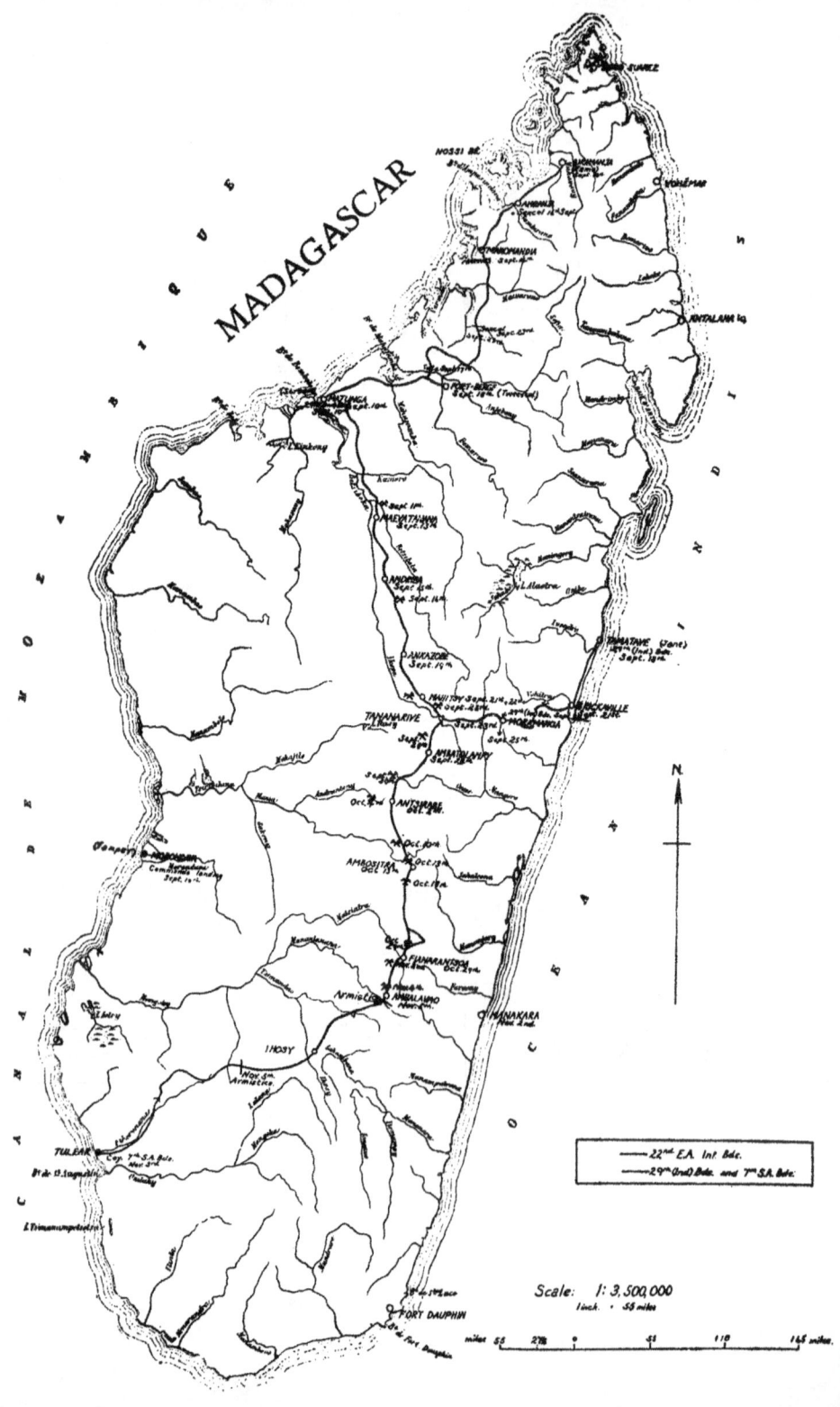

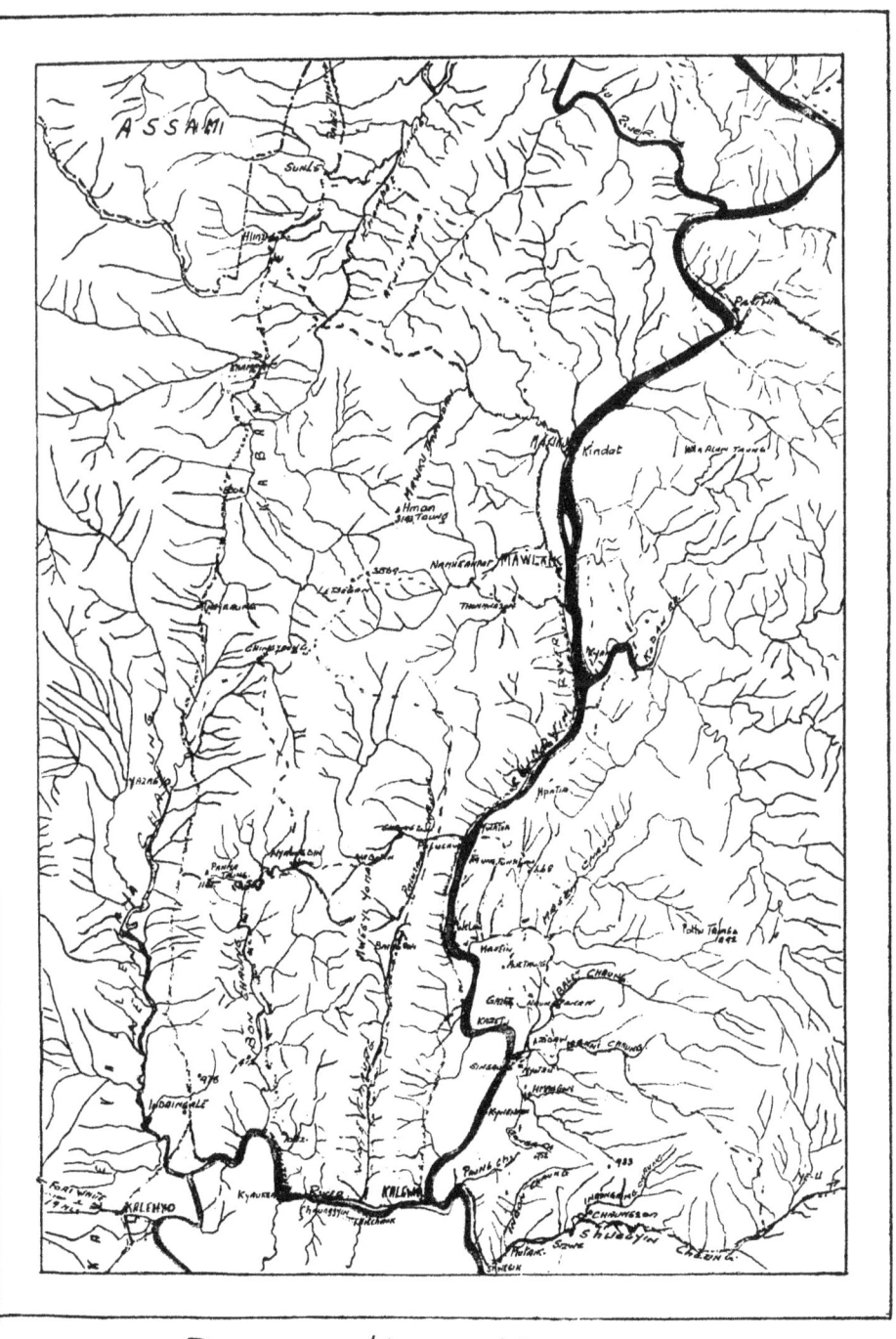

www.ingramcontent.com/pod-product-compliance
Lightning Source LLC
Chambersburg PA
CBHW031148160426
43193CB00008B/289